PSYCHOLOGY
IN THE NURSERY SCHOOL

PSYCHOLOGY IN THE NURSERY SCHOOL

by

NELLY WOLFFHEIM

Former Principal of the Wolffheim-Seminar for
Kindergarten Teachers in Berlin. Honorary
Member of the National Froebel Foundation,
London.

Translated by

CHARLES L. HANNAM

GREENWOOD PRESS, PUBLISHERS
WESTPORT, CONNECTICUT

The Library of Congress has catalogued this publication as follows:

Library of Congress Cataloging in Publication Data

```
Wolffheim, Nelly, 1879-
   Psychology in the nursery school.

   1.  Education, Preschool--1945-       2.  Child
study.  I.  Title.
[LB1140.W6  1972]          372.21'6       77-162630
ISBN 0-8371-6197-5
```

Originally published in 1953
by Philosophical Library, Inc., New York

Reprinted with the permission
of the Philosophical Library, Inc.

First Greenwood Reprinting 1972

Library of Congress Catalogue Card Number 77-162630

ISBN 0-8371-6197-5

Printed in the United States of America

CIP   2 NOV 1972

In memory of the late psychoanalyst
DR. KARL ABRAHAM
who first suggested the writing
of this book

PREFACE

In the following pages I describe my attempts over many years to enlarge the function of the nursery school in accordance with Freud's psychoanalytical (1) findings. It will be shown not only that the nursery school should be run on psychoanalytical lines but also that it can be a source of important material for psychoanalytical research. I believe that the nursery school is capable of doing important work in this respect. The psychoanalytically trained nursery school teacher will not only be able to produce material of importance to psychology thanks to her sharpened powers of observation; but as a result of her practical work she will be able to confirm many of the points which adult analyses have revealed partly by implication and induction. The more teachers and those in charge of children are able to learn from Freud's child psychology the more success they will have in their work with children. The many examples of the nature of child behaviour which I have experienced and describe in this book may be of interest to parents also.

CONTENTS

GLOSSARY OF TERMS

(1) *Psychoanalysis, psychoanalytical pedagogy :* Psychoanalysis, initiated by Freud, in the narrow sense the method of treating psychological illness. In the wider sense it is the depth-psychology founded by him which is used for research in various fields of knowledge. By psychoanalytical pedagogy we understand that system of education which stems from the teachings of Freud.

(2) *Neurotic :* The neurosis is a psychological illness which develops due to inner conflicts, mostly connected with disturbances of the instinctual life.

(3) Vide 6

(4) *Child analysis :* Psychoanalytical therapy suitable for children. There are two main schools of child analysis, one deriving from Anna Freud, the other from Melanie Klein.

(5) *Ego ideal :* It is found in the child as a result of his parents' wishes and other influences of his upbringing. It is the dominant motive in the child's moral development.

(6) *Repression :* Affects, images, wishes, also memories of experiences are repressed into the unconscious if the personality is unable to bear them (its ego ideal).

(7) *Symptom :* Pathological symptom often masking the real unconscious cause.

(8) *Inhibitions :* Prohibitions imposed on oneself, usually without being conscious of having done so.

(9) *Instinctual renunciation :* Renunciation of the gratification of an instinct.

(10) *To overcompensate :* To keep an emotion better

repressed, the opposite emotion is over emphasised. Example: in place of hate originally present, an over-strong affection appears.

(11) *Mistake (Parapraxis)*: Starting from the assumption that in the mind nothing happens by chance, psychoanalysis regards small, apparently trivial remarks and actions, such as slips of the tongue, lapses of memory, seemingly random movements, dropping and breaking as involuntary representations of psychic states.

(12) *Œdipus Complex*: A complex is a group of thoughts and emotions, emotionally linked, centring around a focal point. The Œdipus Complex refers to the strong sexually toned emotional tie of the child to one of his parents—usually one of the opposite sex—which usually appears in the first few years of life and can often entail a rejection, bordering on hate, of the other parent. The Œdipus myth symbolises this conflict.

(13) *The passing of the Œdipus Complex*: At about the fifth year the emotional intensity lessens, and at this stage the Œdipus Complex becomes repressed.

(14) *Sublimation*: The redirection of asocial instinctual expression and sexual desires that cannot be fulfilled in socially adjusted activity.

(15) *Transference*: Emotional relationships—originally meant for someone else—are "transferred" to a substitute person. It does not become conscious that it is only a case of transferred emotion (either affection or dislike), not of a spontaneous feeling.

(16) *Ambivalence*: Two-sidedness of emotion, the contemporaneous existence of love and hate.

(17) *Trauma*: Emotional injury with lasting damaging effects. Experiences of terror, profound hurts, disappointments, etc.

(18) *Super-Ego* : An agency which operates in the unconscious as controller and supervisor of the actions and intentions of the ego, carrying out the functions of censor.

(19) *Identification* : To act or to feel as a whole, or in certain traits, like someone else; to absorb him so to speak as a whole or partially within oneself.

(20) *Castration Complex* : The emotional reaction connected with the often unconscious fear of losing the genitals.

(21) *Masculinity Complex* : Dissatisfaction of the woman with her sexual role, often present unconsciously.

(22) *Anal* : The word derives from "anus", i.e., pertaining to the anus.

(23) *Symbol* : Form of expression of a cause that has remained in the unconscious. Symbolic figures: personalities to which certain symbolically expressed feelings refer.

(24) *Pleasure-Ego* : The child seeks gratification of his desires only, i.e., he wants only what gives him pleasure.

(25) *Regression* : Withdrawal to an earlier stage of development.

(26) *Narcissistic* : In love with oneself.

(27) *Sadistic* : Taking pleasure in making others suffer.

(28) *Phobia* : Pathologically heightened fear, usually of an occasion in which fear is engendered.

(29) *Latent* : Hidden, restricted. Particularly with reference to the cessation and retrogression of sexual development from six to eight years onwards—latency period.

CHAPTER I

BASIC IDEAS OF PSYCHOANALYTICAL EDUCATION IN A NURSERY SCHOOL

Freud has shown us the connection between early experiences and later neurotic (2) complaints and has known how to deduce the development of the personality from occurrences hitherto ignored. The influence of unconscious (3) mental processes on the thoughts and actions of a person must also be considered in relation to the behaviour of the child and its teachers. Those who have once acquainted themselves with psycho-analytical theories, and especially those who have in addition paid attention to the psychological results made available by child-analysis (4), will find great difficulty in reconciling the educational principles formerly valid with the new point of view.

The most important point that has been made is that psychoanalytical education has done away with the idealised concept of the "good" child. It must be emphasised that the "good child" merely adds to the comfort of the teacher, but is fundamentally an unhealthy phenomenon which may have a disadvantageous influence on the later character development of the person. Although modern educational theory has in any case tended to lessen the favourable view held of being "good", the inter-connection and deeper implication of the dangers to which the child trained to be "good" is exposed have been shown to us only by psychoanalysis.

Let us observe in what manner the "goodness" of the child comes into being. A small child will come to obey the orders of grown-ups for three main reasons. Either we can make the child obey by fear—a method that has been rejected by the conscientious educator for a long time. Or the child obeys from love, because it wants to please grown-ups. It then endeavours to reach the ideal which its beloved parents place before it. The wish to be like either father or mother acts as a driving force. Thus an ego-ideal (5) is formed which the child attempts to reach. If the ego-ideal is very powerful in the child it will attempt to suppress everything within itself that is not in accordance with the ideal it is trying to reach. Those drives and wishes will be suppressed which to the child seem forbidden because of the attitude of those around it, or because of repeatedly expressed prohibitions. Psychoanalytical experience has shown, however, that the healthy development of the child may be hindered by too strong repression (6). Faulty emotional development and even physical symptoms (7) frequently originate from this. All kinds of inhibitions (8) capable of strangling the joy of living, self-confidence and the urge to be active, may have arisen merely because the child lost the battle with the demands made on him and his own efforts to reach his ego-ideal. Feelings of guilt, which play an important part in the lives of all men may increase to an exaggerated extent in these circumstances, making the child feel inferior.

In recognition of such facts educators should avoid making too severe demands on any child. We should regard instinctual renunciation (9) as a necessity and demand an adaptation to reality from the child, but avoid exaggerating these demands.

A further incentive to behave according to the parents' wishes is the child's inherent urge to develop, to be like grown-ups. This is an important foundation for all the child's endeavours, probably not known to himself but clearly recognisable by the observer. When we work against this drive by undermining the child's urge to independence, by mollycoddling him too long and helping him unnecessarily, we delay his development. We prevent him from growing out of the baby stage at the right time and instead of advancing, we delay his progress. In a later chapter we shall see what may lie behind such behaviour on the part of those in charge of children.

An important part of Freud's discoveries is the recognition of human frailty even in the child. He is not as good and free from fault as we liked to believe from our own wishful imaginings. Freud's depth psychology has taught us that words and deeds often have quite different unconscious motives behind them to those which appear on the surface. We know now that (for example) excessive kindness, an exaggerated urge to cleanliness and similar characteristics, which have always filled the hearts of teachers with joy, frequently cover the opposite character-traits in reality (over-compensation) (10). Strong egotistic tendencies may operate in the unconscious of a particularly self-sacrificing child and may not take effect because of their repression. They upset the child, however, and may one day break through with the greatest intensity, to everyone's surprise.

In this connection it is not unimportant to mention Therese Simon's *The Dual Existence of the Child* (*Das Doppelleben des Kindes*).* She is thinking not only of unconscious reactions when she writes as follows about the well-adjusted child who tends to compromise:

"Thus the child has no alternative but to submit outwardly to the adjustments demanded of him and to swal-

* T. Simon. *Das Doppelleben des Kindes.* Rotapfel Verlag, Eulebach Zuerich, 1937, p. 58–59.

low his rebellious feelings. From then onwards he shows grown-ups a façade of well-adjusted behaviour. As this façade corresponds to what grown-ups wish to see, they are only too easily inclined to mistake it for the child's real behaviour—whereas inwardly he is raging with rebellion.''

Instead of suppressing with severity everything that seems to us undesirable in the child, psychoanalytical education tries to canalise the undesirable urge in a socially useful manner. Thus—to give an example— instead of punishing a dirty child who has the urge to grub about in mud, the tendency to like dirt is recognised as appropriate to this stage of this individual child's development. Therefore an attempt is made to give useful expression to his urge to play about with dirt and the child is given paints, sand and water to play with, and plasticine until a more conscious creativeness arises out of the primitive urge. (Later this subject will be treated in more detail.)

Above all psychoanalytical education takes account of the child's wishes and desires, and recognises the magnitude of the task in front of him, namely to adjust himself to reality. Therefore the child's urges are only suppressed when external circumstances demand this. This does not seem to us like mollycoddling but the path to free development. To the psychoanalytically-minded educator repression that is too strong means inhibition, which may lead to the repression of rebellious feelings, the accumulation of affects and the formation of hatreds. All these states of mind will have a detri-mental influence on the emotional development of the child. Thus educational interference from those in charge of the child should be reduced without, however, being entirely rejected.

We must try to discover above all the unconscious

causes of the obstacles which the child puts in the way of his own education. If we are sufficiently trained in this direction, the child's general behaviour, his mistakes (11), and above all his play, which is an expression of his emotional life, may be of help as indications.

It is well known that psychoanalysis has revealed the existence of the child's sexuality. We can now take account of the new discoveries in the running of the nursery school and, as will be seen later, pay attention to facts that have been overlooked previously.

Lastly the following should be emphasised. It is known to-day that the behaviour of children is governed by emotional factors which frequently remain untouched by the influence of deliberate educational measures. It is known that neurotic children exist who, through their own troubles, make their education troublesome. We know of children whose adjustment to reality has never been achieved and who therefore have come into conflict with the external world where a sensible attitude to education makes attempts to avoid unnecessary conflicts. It is a well-known fact to-day that so-called problem children have often only become difficult because their parents or those in charge of them are themselves badly adjusted and suffer from emotional or neurotic problems. We must therefore be more modest, both in the degree of adjustment we demand from the child and in our belief in our own infallibility. We must, however, make more serious demands on ourselves and examine our own behaviour more closely.

The lessons to be learnt by those in charge of nursery schools, arising out of the few ideas briefly sketched here, will be seen in the following chapters. Our most immediate task is to describe the stage of the child's development by the time it is old enough to go to the nursery school.

CHAPTER II

STAGES OF DEVELOPMENT
IN THE NURSERY SCHOOL AND THE TASKS
ARISING OUT OF THIS

The manifestations of the Œdipus Complex (12) *in the
nursery school.*

In the nursery school we often have to deal with
children in whom the Œdipus Complex has reached its
climax; and we may also count on the passing of the
Œdipus Complex (13) during the time the child is in
the nursery school. In the realisation that the children
are in the midst of a struggle and that they are passing
through a vitally important stage of their development,
the nursery school teacher must attempt to keep harmful
influences out of their way and to afford them some
relief. The children must be helped in their difficulties
by being offered the possibility of sublimation (14)
—finding substitutive satisfaction for their wishes.

Experience has shown that with some children difficulties are released when visiting the nursery school—
especially at the beginning—which seem to arise out of
the natural conflicts of this age group. The fact that
difficulties of this kind do not arise as frequently as we
might expect according to our theories, seems some proof
to me that the nursery school is able to provide a desirable alternative for most children and that it can help
the child in his conflicts. We must of course beware of
drawing conclusions only from the outward behaviour
of the child, as it is well known that a great deal more

happens in the unconscious emotional life than outwardly appears. But as long as no further material from child analysis is available which might allow insight into the child's unconscious reaction to the nursery school, it is necessary to rely on simple observation.

In the first place two questions must be asked: How do the phenomena resulting from the Œdipus Complex become evident in the nursery school, and on what is the assumption based that the nursery school may be able to offer the child help in this conflict?

According to my experiences the child's difficulties are expressed mostly by his overall pattern of behaviour. Strongly neurotic children reveal irritability, excitability and often also anxiety symptoms, which, it might be assumed, are connected with the Œdipus situation. For example the five-year-old Sonja in my nursery school was always in a bad mood and had great need of affection whenever her father was away on one of his frequent journeys. This was very noticeable. During those times she was always rebellious, contradicted everything, deliberately did what she was not supposed to do, did not occupy herself properly, and played the fool with the other children; while a chronic stomachic disorder became worse during these periods. This state of affairs continued until her father returned from his travels. Before long we needed no information about the father's whereabouts, Sonja's behaviour being a sure indication. The strong emotional attachment of the child to her father was clearly pronounced.

Three-year-old Heinz also gave clear proof of an Œdipus attachment. He was very surly when his father fetched him from the nursery school, but greeted his mother with passionate caresses. This child had behaved quite normally in the nursery school for several

months and was the favourite of all other children because of his charm. Then a sudden change in his behaviour took place, he became more and more difficult,
bad-tempered and irritable. Finally we had to recognise
that an acute neurosis had broken out. A disappointment caused by his mother, whom he loved very much,
was the basis of his illness.

Many examples could be given as further evidence of
the effects of the Œdipus Complex. It also seems worth
noting that many children behave quite differently in
the nursery school to the way they do at home. Those
children who cause the greatest amount of trouble at
home are often well adjusted in the nursery school,
capable of self denial and able to comply with the demands made on them there. For example FRITZ, who
gave the impression of being remarkably sensible for his
five years, who was always open to reason, who never
reacted violently to a prohibition or any restriction of
his freedom, was furiously violent towards his mother
at home. The strength of an otherwise weakly child
became so great during his tantrums that his mother
was unable to hold him and had to flee from his blows.
It does not seem credible that faulty upbringing alone
was the cause of such behaviour. It would not be mistaken to conclude that it was unsatisfied love of the
mother engendered by the Œdipus Complex which
made the child react in such a manner only to her. We
do know that conflicts originating in the home environment disappear in the nursery school, but we must remember that other conflicts are possible there. If
children who are difficult at home are often easily controlled in the nursery school and do not exhibit their
home behaviour there, we must conclude that neither
character traits nor a "nervous disposition" of the child

can be the cause of its behaviour at home, but rather family relationships as such. We pointed out earlier what a strong impression one often gets of the difficulties of a child's domestic environment, and there is no doubt that neurotic parents unconsciously foster the neuroses of their children. Too much or too little love, unpredictable changes in the parent's attitude, too much pampering, or the exaggerated application of a "toughening-up" process—physical or mental—are especially found in neurotic families. Unsatisfactory relationships between husband and wife, induce many a mother to seek an outlet for her emotions in one child, thereby attaching it too much to herself.*

Frequently domestic emotional attitudes are transferred to the new environment, but if we are able to evaluate them as transferences, (15) our own reactions will be less emotionally coloured than they would be between parents and children. As soon as the teacher has learned to view the child's love and hate, its jealousy and claims for recognition, its rebelliousness and its need for affection as part of the process of transference—that is, to treat it impersonally—the guidance of the child will transcend immediate personal relations.

In psychoanalysis there are the concepts of "positive" and "negative" transference, that is emotions of love and of rejection. Let us take the case of FRIEDEL (aged 6) who quite clearly demonstrated her attitude of rejection one day, though in general she was very attached to me. On a walk the child told me the following daydream. She pointed out a tower and mentioned

---

* It seems to me sensible that children are only accepted for treatment in English Child Guidance Clinics if the mothers, and sometimes the fathers also, undertake to come to the clinic for advice on problems of the child's upbringing, or, where necessary, even for some kind of psychological treatment for themselves.

to me in a friendly voice that she wished to hang me from it. She gave a most detailed account of this procedure, visibly enjoying her cruelty in relating to me how I would hang from up there in a most uncomfortable position. The child showed no kind of excitement during this conversation and could not give any reason for her plan. It is not at all unusual for children who are used to "free conversation" to relieve their unconscious emotions in daydreams. In this case it was not hard for me to find the deeper reason for FRIEDEL'S temporary resentment with some degree of certainty. The child was involved in strong emotional conflicts in its home. She was attached to her father to an exaggerated degree and apparently recognised the unsatisfactory relations of her parents to one another. In her mother she recognised the severe and forbidding authority, which seemed even more pronounced in contrast to her father's pampering. Rarely has the Œdipus Complex of a child been so clearly revealed to me as in this case. FRIEDEL was filled with love for her father and jealous hate of her mother. I had to suppose that the imaginary punishment inflicted was meant for the mother and not for me—for, as far as I could recollect, I had given no cause for such strong resentment—and that the hatred had been transferred to me on the spur of the moment This appeared to be confirmed when the father of the child told me afterwards, that FRIEDEL had that very morning witnessed a quarrel between her parents, during which she had taken sides against her mother.

We must never forget the duality of emotions which causes love and hate to exist close to one another. The opposition of contemporaneous emotions—in psychoanalysis the term "ambivalence" (16) is used—is especially strong and natural in children. Therefore, one should never adopt a moral attitude towards statements of this kind by children. We must cease to be horrified by these apparently cruel and unfeeling daydreams, or perhaps even to assume pathological depravity in conversations such as the one mentioned above. Particularly at the age while the child is at the nursery school—a time which demands so much renunciation of urges and resolution of inner conflicts—must we not be surprised by unpredictable changes in behaviour. The knowledge of the transference of emotions can help us to face the results of "positive" and "negative" expressions of these emotions with understanding.

In order to avoid misunderstandings it should be emphasised that the possibility of a transferred emotional relation should not prevent us from examining our own attitude to the children, and we should ask ourselves in each individual case whether we have given any cause for resentment and irritation, or for an excess of love.

In order to understand the emotional condition of the individual child it is most important to observe its behaviour closely from the moment it enters the nursery school. That is the point at which one can discover most clearly the state of the child's development. An exaggeratedly painful separation from the mother points to too close a relation between mother and child in most cases. Then special attention should be paid to grief, shown in the form of anxious clinging to adults, also to bad temper and to emotional weeping, especially if the child is not to be counted among the timid, the inhibited or the shy, according to the general impression it gives or to its mother's account of it. The greatest caution is necessary in these cases, as an emotion connected with the Œdipus Complex may be involved—

that is, the child may be experiencing an event which may easily develop into a trauma (17). Frequently, however, fear is not revealed outwardly and is visible only to the trained eye. Self-assured behaviour may be the cover for anxiety. Emmanuel Klein (New York) discusses the various reasons which may lie behind the fear of going to school in a very suggestive essay. We shall not go very far wrong if we assume that the same reasons underlie the fear of the nursery school. "All the child's fears, anxieties, self-consciousness, feelings of inadequacy, his relations to his parents, to his siblings and to himself, tend to be reflected in the school situation. The symptoms associated with school distress range from the physically expressed anticipatory anxiety— symptoms such as morning sickness, vomiting, diarrhœa, abdominal cramps, great difficulty in getting up in the morning which often vanishes magically in the holidays —to disorders in learning and behaviour in the classroom."*

Since these connections became clear to me I went ahead with the process of getting the children used to the nursery school much more carefully and cautiously whenever there were any signs of difficulty. There was to be no strict ignoring, no distractions or novelties to help the child to forget. Instead there had to be sympathetic behaviour on the teacher's part, and if possible the continued presence of the mother, if this seemed necessary to me and the child did not wish to stay on its own. Only when the attraction of the community life of the nursery school is effective enough to overcome the child's sadness at parting, anxiety, or the wrench of being

---

* E. Klein. "The reluctance to go to school". *The Psychoanalytical Study of the Child*, I, 1945, p. 263, Imago Publishing Co. Ltd., London.

left behind by its mother, only then should the child stay in the nursery school on its own.*

If we effect the separation too energetically in cases where a child shows hostility or fear towards the nursery school, if it is jealous of younger brothers or sisters who can now remain with the mother, if it thinks that from now onwards it will have to be always alone, we shall achieve the opposite of what we aim at by having the child in the nursery school: instead of social adjustment, hostility and increased withdrawal, instead of help, the multiplication of existing difficulties.

Melanie Klein mentions that the psychoanalysis of children frequently reveals the fear, though in varying degrees, of being sent away from home as a punishment. This fear begins at a very early stage and may be a heavy burden on the child's mind.† Even if this discovery is not directly concerned with the nursery school, we should bear it in mind in any case of a strong and inexplicable fear.

If it is impossible to accustom the child to the nursery school for a long time—actually a problem that arises very infrequently—I am in favour of stopping the experiment and making it again at a later date when the child's emotional condition is more favourable. If another attempt is made the nursery school visited the first time should not be chosen again; not because the school has failed, for in most cases it is not to blame, but be-

---

* There are cases, of course, in which the immediate accommodation of the child is absolutely necessary and *gradual acclimatisation difficult*. These should not prevent us from emphasising what appears to us the most advisable. It would pay to try to help the child even if the external factors force us to ignore the psychological problems. If symptoms continue, it is recommended that the child should be taken to a Child Guidance Clinic.

† Melanie Klein and Joan Riviere, *Love, Hate and Reparation*, p. 109, Hogarth Press and Institute of Psychoanalysis, London, 1937·

cause the child's mental picture of it is bound up with unpleasant memories. Previous association of ideas may work against new impressions which the child may otherwise be ready to receive. Of course any child can gradually be brought round to an outward conformity; but one just does not know to what dangers its emotional balance may be exposed. Besides we must not forget that a constant and continuing fear of the nursery school may cause far-reaching difficulties when the child attends schools in later life. In relation to this problem special caution is needed for an orphaned child or one who has lost either a father or mother. It is burdened by impressions which the group life of the nursery school may ease but which may, on the other hand, be revived anew. Children may live again through an anxiety once experienced if they are suddenly left alone in the nursery school. Children who have known the tragic experience of a sudden loss may react to the separation from their home with anxiety attacks. It is recommended that the person responsible for the education of the child should have this possibility pointed out when the child is brought to the nursery school, so that the first day there should not be a shock to it.

The privations of a child who has lost its mother are usually evaluated correctly, but the fatherless child also lives under difficulties which are not taken into account sufficiently in most cases. It is thought merely that the male influence and control are lacking, but there is more to it than that: there is both the loss of a close relative, a personality who gave emotional stability, and the incomprehensible nature of the whole event. The psychoanalysis of children has shown that external indifference often hides the most acute suffering and a deeply felt longing for the return of the lost parent.

Stages of Development in the Nursery

Some of the peculiar behaviour of such children, their bad adjustment to group life and many other deviations from the normal may be related to the situation in the child's family. Their different position in comparison with other children may by itself raise problems for orphaned children. The subconscious of such children may be profoundly disturbed by the incomprehensible fact of having less than others, though they may never question this fact. The mental and physical problems of a widowed mother in relation to her child must also be taken into account. She burdens the child, which is for her a substitute, with a too possessive love through her own loneliness, as frequently as she may spoil the atmosphere in the home with her bitter moods and lack of emotional warmth. The too conscientious mother who wishes to take the father's place by imposing a strict discipline is also in some cases not without danger to a passionate, anxious child.* Can the nursery school help these children to cope with the real difficulties in their lives, and can the child find something there of what has been destroyed for it? In many cases the friendly, gay atmosphere of the nursery school may perhaps give the endangered child a new direction and purpose in life and may ease the burden on its mind. This must not, however, consist of forgetting or repressing what it has lived through, but of relieving a burden which the home environment may be incapable of relieving. If the child is happy in the nursery school and manages to find substitutive satisfaction for emotions that have been lying fallow so far, much will have been achieved. An understanding nursery school teacher will do everything to help the child to find a resolution of its difficul-

* See Susan Isaacs. *From Fatherless Children.* New Education Fellowship Monograph No. 2, 1945.

ties. The way for this will be found in uninhibited conversation, in the child's play, and its drawings. The greater the extent to which the intelligent co-operation of the child's relatives, those responsible for its education or its foster mother can be secured, the more easily will it be possible for the nursery school also to fulfil its task in this direction.

Unconscious opposition to the nursery school, probably based on jealousy, causes many a mother, even under normal conditions, to increase the emotional ties of the child to herself and the family. Instead of helping the child they increase his difficulties in adapting himself to a new group. The observer will notice the mother's unconscious negative attitude even when she seems outwardly in favour of the nursery school, either in the child's interest or to ease her own domestic burden. The opposition of conscious and unconscious tendencies in our emotional lives is given expression even in situations like this. Frequently a sympathetic attitude on the part of the nursery school teacher is necessary here in order to intervene helpfully. We know that it is difficult to fight a mother's opposition arising out of her own complexes. It has struck me that boys are more often inseparably attached to their mothers. The supposition lies close at hand that on both sides the effects of an Œdipus situation are becoming apparent.

Generally the period of getting used to the nursery school goes surprisingly well. The new surroundings give the children distraction, new acquaintances, stimulating activities, in short, sources of pleasure of a varying nature which also enable subconscious instinctual demands to be directed into new channels. During this period the new surroundings can be a useful help to the child. On the basis of repeated observation one can assume that the child is released, to a certain extent, from previous preoccupation with himself and his own wishes. He finds the opportunity to offer up his love to others and to transfer his desires, previously directed solely towards his parents, to other people. Living in a group in which each child is equally placed, the sexual urges influencing the child can be sublimated. We must regard it as desirable and perhaps consider it one of the most important tasks of the nursery school that we provide a wider sphere for the range of the child's interests and emotions. We thus work against a too-prolonged and exclusive attachment to the parents. Presumably the passing of the Œdipus Complex is made more difficult, if no other influences helping the child to reorientate himself are offered.

It is true that most unenlightened parents consider it highly desirable to have their child strongly attached to them. They proudly talk of their devoted child, which would rather be only with them and only play with them. Such recognition usually hides the desire of the parents, due to their own fixation, to keep the child entirely for themselves. This influence on the child may cause it lasting damage because its super-ego (18) takes the praise as guidance and reinforces the attachment between parents and child still further. Obstacles are placed in the course of the child's free and natural development which may bring difficulties for the rest of its life. "If in our earliest development we have been able to transfer our interest and love from our mother to other people and other sources of gratification, then, only then, are we able in later life to derive enjoyment from a wide range."*

* Melanie Klein and Joan Riviere. *Love, Hate and Reparation*, p. 118.

Psychology in the Nursery School

Particularly in the case of only children must we be aware of the danger of an excessive attachment. There are many opportunities to observe the effects of such attachments in the nursery school. The pampering usually lavished on an only child, the sole possession of all it loves, the absence of any struggle for the parents' love arising from the rivalry between brothers and sisters—all this goes to make the ties with the family especially lasting, and to keep the child dependent. The late August Aichhorn* has illustrated the difficult condition into which an only child is brought by a short-sighted mother. She spoils the child in every respect, allows far too much gratification of his wishes, but is, on the other hand, because of her own timidity, all too ready to inhibit the child and to arrest his development by superfluous prohibitions. The child is faced with a muddled, and for him, incomprehensible, situation by these indulgences and prohibitions. Reality with its irrevocable demands can finally be hidden from the child no longer. Demands which are gradually made on the child in a normal education and are coped with gradually are suddenly imposed with intense urgency.

As we have seen, the nursery school should help the child with the task of freeing itself from its early surroundings. It may save an only child from a lifelong dependency. For real emotional detachment to be possible it is indeed essential that there should be no continuing neurotic attachment such as can hardly be affected from without—except by an influence on the subconscious, such as is assured by psychoanalysis. A nursery school can, however, only be a help if it is conceived on the right lines. If a child is placed in a large

* A. Aichhorn. *Wayward Youth.* Imago Publishing Co. Ltd. London, 1951.

nursery school, the transference is made more difficult, as the conditions for close contact with his nursery school teacher or for friendships with other children are not favourable there. The same must be said of the old style nursery schools, in which free play and free movement were rarely customary and most of the time was spent in sitting still and being occupied with communal tasks. This disadvantage of large or unfavourably organised nursery schools has, so far as I know, not been pointed out yet; but if, as I have so far sought to show, the liberation of the child from its close family ties is one of the tasks of the nursery school, we must not ignore this point.

CHAPTER III

EFFECTS ON COMMUNITY LIFE OF THE RELATIONSHIPS BETWEEN BROTHERS AND SISTERS

The emotional conditions revealed by psychoanalysis have taught us the importance of the relations of an individual with his brothers and sisters. Earlier educational theory took no notice of these facts or did not find them important enough to pay attention to them. We, however, have learnt to recognise that the eldest, the one in the middle, and also the youngest child of a family, are each exposed to possibilities of conflict because of their peculiar position. This position is capable of influencing the formation of the child's character and its attitude to life. Jealousy and competition, feelings of inferiority arising out of the inability to keep pace with the others, the fear of not receiving enough love, arrogance and the desire to dominate may arise while brothers and sisters live together and cannot be easily removed even where an attempt is consciously made to counter them by educational endeavour. We find enlightenment on this state of affairs in psychoanalytical literature. Of special importance is any information which instructs us about the normal grudge of girls against boys and illuminates the early thought given by children to sex differences.* We must assume,

* The following should be mentioned: S. Freud. *Introductory Lectures on Psychoanalysis*, p. 280–281. George Allen & Unwin, Ltd., London. Hug.-Hellmuth, *Aus dem Seelenleben des Kindes*, 2nd Edn. Vienna, 1921, p. 128. Wittels, *Die Befreiung des Kindes*, Hippocrates Verlag, Stuttgart, 1927, Ch. VI.

and have some evidence for doing so, that the conflicts experienced among brothers and sisters reappear if the child is removed to another group of children. A great deal of what has been suppressed at home or has been overcompensated for there, finds an opportunity to come to the surface.

The only child who has to share his possessions for the first time in the nursery school and is suddenly faced by the necessity of having to assert himself, will have many difficulties until he has achieved the necessary degree of acclimatisation. The only child experiences rivalry between brothers and sisters for the first time in the nursery school, while for the others it is more in the nature of an extension or repetition of home experiences. The only child, previously the established centre point of its environment, is now one of many.*

Our brief discussion of the individual difficulties of children has made us realise that each child comes to the nursery school with an attitude to it arising out of his personal problems. Now bearing this fact in mind let us see whether among these small children there is any sort of community spirit. Everywhere, and especially in the Montessori Kinderhaus, development of community sense and guidance towards social consciousness are considered the primary aims of education. Of course we also wish to guide the child towards other children, as all our efforts are made to enable it to cope with reality and we want it to achieve a secure position in the community. But before the child can become

* Only children who are going to have a brother or sister should be sent to a nursery school in good time, not only when the second child is born and the firstborn already considers himself to have lost his privileges and be neglected. He must take root in the school and must be made to lose his self-centred outlook; above all the emotional ties with his mother must be loosened a little in preparation, so that he is better prepared for the coming danger of conflict.

35

attached to the group he must become attached to the person in charge of the nursery school, and a good relation between the latter and the child will lead to this. For the purpose of discussing the question of group education, it seems to me of no great importance whether the nursery school teacher gives expression to the maternal family principle, although this seems the right one to me, or whether she takes the part of a detached teaching guide (Montessori). What is however essential is a personality able to focus the interest of the children upon herself.

This is what Freud has to say about the origins of the community spirit. He holds that the self-abnegation demanded by the majority will be made easier by renunciation and identification (19) with the others. "No one must want to put himself forward, everyone must be the same and have the same. Social justice means that we deny ourselves many things so that others may have to do without them as well, or, what is the same thing, may not be able to ask for them. The demand for equality is the root of social conscience and the sense of duty."* Being equals in the eyes of the person in charge binds the children to her; fundamentally each child wants to see, consciously or unconsciously, a beloved mother in her, or in any case an object that it can identify as personally belonging to it. Like brothers and sisters the fellow members of the school are rivals with whom one has to fight for supremacy. It can be observed that although the children manifest their love to the nursery school teacher differently (where they are not prevented by a too-authoritative manner) some are in greater need of a close relationship with her than others. But if we

---

* Freud. *Group Psychology and the Analysis of the Ego.* International Psychoanalytical Press. London-Vienna. 1922. p. 88.

are going to speak of living together in a group, she must be for each one the focal point of the nursery school. "Thus social feeling is based on the reversal of what was first a hostile feeling into a positively toned tie of the nature of identification. So far as we have hitherto been able to follow the course of events, this reversal appears to be effected under the influence of a common tender tie with a person outside the group."*

Looking at the development of the community spirit in this way, it will be obvious that the child will only become one of the group willingly, if his relation to the person in charge of the nursery school is a sufficiently strong one, and provided that it has developed by the child's own free will and not by undesirable external pressure. Frequently of course the formal education the child has experienced at home will give the acclimatisation the appearance of having speedily occurred. However, it must be emphasised here that teachers must beware of believing that they can achieve easy successes with children. It is a fault of nearly all educators to believe that their aims are too easily attained; they do not take into account what is taking place in the unconscious of the child behind his conscious emotional life and its manifestations. Observation and the material obtained by child-analysis prove how basically alien the community is to the nature of the small child. It always seeks ties to single individuals even in the larger circle. Where early—that is, unusual—social consciousness, self-denial and considerable interest in the welfare of the group become noticeable, I have nearly always had to recognise these as an overcompensation of strongly anti-social tendencies, which usually came to the surface unexpectedly with great force. Even in the early school

* op. cit., p. 34, pp. 88–89.

age, joining the group will only be an external act and will rarely be fulfilling an inner need. The egocentric orientation of the child can only be changed and gradually reduced after it has been diverted from an excessive interest in his own experiences. As we have seen, the nursery school can and should effect the first step in this process; also it helps to pave the child's way to an easier adjustment to reality in this context. It should, however, be remembered that too much group spirit must not be expected from children in the nursery school stage, at any rate not more than is absolutely necessary to make them a unit.

In a collection of the researches of study groups by the Home and School Council of Great Britain called *Advances in Understanding the Child* (1st Edn. 1935, 4th, 1939) one reads in Henry Wilson's paper on "Willingness to Help": "The child's realisation of himself as a member of a community: this can only come gradually on a foundation of security, based on love, based on the assurance that he has to earn his place in the family circle. The child should not feel that he has to earn his place in the community through acts of helpfulness."

I have gained the impression that most nursery schools have a wrong attitude to the problem of the group spirit. Children are encouraged to make sacrifices which are not easy for them, absolute subordination and considerateness are expected and seeming conformity is taken to mean real inner social adjustment. This assumption emerges especially in reports from the Montessori schools (Kinderhäuser). According to my own experiences and psychoanalytical knowledge we should not let ourselves be too easily deceived by "good" behaviour in children, if in any case we attach much importance to introducing and guiding such young children to some sort of group spirit. With regard to the usual ethical education we must first of all agree whether it is right to concentrate on this at all. Even if the ability for self-sacrifice and self-denial in individual children, and the maximum adjustment to the group, make the running of the nursery school easier, it seems to me that the development of such ethical characteristics is of little value for the child itself. An apparently successful attitude towards the group usually derives merely from an influence arising out of the general tone of the nursery school, and may easily lead the child to suppress its emotions more than is good for it. We have learnt from depth-psychology to appreciate the dangers of excessive repression and should therefore beware of wanting to see the children behave beautifully. The powerful influence spread by the much-loved person in charge of the nursery school must in no case be used to exaggerate the demands made by the child's super-ego. Our demands should be concentrated only on necessities, as the claims of the group are already greater than is to be desired and a too-pointed emphasis on our wishes in this direction is to be avoided.

Therese Simon, drawing attention to the danger inherent in a suggestive educational method gives this important advice: "By bringing the suggestive power of his personality to bear upon the child, the grown-up develops both its inclination and its ability to follow suggestion blindly—i.e., he reinforces and develops the quality of suggestibility. . . . The dependence on suggestion which the adult creates results in the child being later open to all influences and suggestions regardless of their quality."* Both caution and restraint

* Thérèse Simon. *Das Doppelleben des Kindes*, p. 95.

on the part of grown-ups are necessary in the nursery school in recognition of this tendency. A means by which the growing child can be saved from being too easily influenced, is, according to De Mouchy,* the release of its aggressive tendencies against its parents. He explains: "Aggression directed against parents in childhood may produce some useful character traits in later life, e.g., the ability to oppose father figures, to attack authority if it takes the shape of narrow-minded and doctrinaire fanaticism, or to stand up against doctrines or political systems which impose themselves in an authoritarian manner." Already when dealing with small children in the nursery school we should bear this point of view in mind and remember it in our relations with the children and the discipline maintained.

More important for a child's development than its attitude to the nursery school as a whole, I think, is its relationship with one other child. Small groups of friends usually form the foundations of larger circles, unless— as we have to relate elsewhere—separation occurs through some strongly developed erotic tie. Children should find in the nursery school friends who are a substitute for what they lacked at home, or through whom they can make up for their domestic difficulties. A five-year-old boy PETER had enforced his supremacy over all other children in the nursery school, and in a closer friendship with another child he was also dominant. A strict ruler, he seemed to be taking revenge for what he was suffering at home. His elder sister treated him badly and bullied him on every possible occasion. MICHAEL, a six-year-old who was known as the "small brother" at home, gained

* Mentioned by Torsten Ramer, "Aggression in relation to family life". International Conference on Child Psychology, London, August 1948.

self-confidence in the nursery school because he was one of the oldest. Single children often compensate for their longing for a brother or sister by friendship with another child, even though we must assume that a loving attitude to another, often younger child masks an over-compensated hate and fear, frequently uncovered in analysis, of a brother or sister as yet unborn.

"Fears of possible rivals are active in all children from an early age. They arise in part from the child's earliest rivalries and hostilities in regard to the parents and from phantasies of loss of the mother's love or punishment from the father's anger. Such fears are strengthened by the child's occasional contacts with visiting children or with new babies in other homes."*

When we observe isolation from others in children, the desire to interfere authoritatively is certainly mistaken. It should be our task to give the children occasion to find friendships by letting them be together without restraint. Artificial introductions of children who seem suited to one another may easily be harmful. I know of a case of this kind which may prove instructive. A small girl was rejected by a larger group of children, or at any rate believed herself to be unwelcome to others. She was officially introduced to the children and was made to join one of their games; as a grown-up woman she could still describe the agonies she had suffered when forced to do this. She kept this fear of being a burden to others, which this childhood experience had created, or at least reinforced, until this fear—among others— was removed by psychoanalysis in later life.

Isolation through the child's own choice is probably always connected with forces at work in the unconscious,

* S. Isaacs. *The Nursery Years*. Routledge, London. 1942 Edition, p. 90.

and external influence alone will seldom be able to achieve much. Sometimes the child gradually sorts himself out and discovers how to find a way to join the group. A relation with one child is frequently the bridge to others.* Where the isolation continues, it should be noted and evaluated in connection with the child's general behaviour. If the tendency to isolate itself continues, the help of a psychologist may be considered unless we ourselves are able to solve the child's problem in a friendly conversation.

It seems questionable to me whether artificially organised communal interests, such as projects for nature study undertaken by a group of children, can really contribute towards welding children into a community. More will be said about this when occupations in the nursery school are discussed; all that should be pointed out here is the danger of regarding this question too much from the outside. Children even in a small group are exposed to influences that cannot be apprehended by us, and they can only be made to conform by force. Is it not characteristic of the younger child in the nursery school to play on its own if left to its own devices? The three-year-old is still far too much concerned with his own ego and has rarely the ability to imagine himself in the place of other children and to picture their play fantasies. The wish for a community of interests comes only gradually; then communal games chosen by the children themselves may really serve to bind the children to one another.

The help that can be given to children in the nursery school by enabling them to cope with their family conflicts and to make the necessary adjustment to reality, has already been pointed out. A further important

* See the paragraph about the friendship of children.

point remains to be mentioned. We know that the only child has to suffer more in the process of education than do members of a family, partly because the parents' urge to educate (*Erziehungszwang*) is entirely concentrated on the one child, partly because prohibitions and commands and all the sacrifices connected with these are much more noticeable to the only child. We must here remember the saying "A trouble shared is a trouble halved" and apply it to the situation of the child. If the child sees that others have to obey along with him, he suffers less from the renunciation and views educational measures less as a personal punishment. It may be assumed that the fact that some children are more easily guided in the nursery school than at home is also connected with this. In addition, as one knows, children educate one another. They sometimes identify themselves with each other and form an alliance against the education forced upon them by authority. Quarrels among themselves have not nearly the same effect on children as conflicts with grown-ups, which are disappointments—disappointments in love—to the child.* In this we find a good argument for the outwardly passive behaviour of the teacher which is recommended by Maria Montessori. Let us leave it to the children to the greatest possible extent to find their own bearings in the community and to let themselves be educated by it. Susan Isaacs also is of the opinion that however good our relation to the child, by the simple fact that we are adults, we exert too great a "pressure" on it. With other children a child can express his fantasy world in his games. In their communal games the children gain real experience of social relations. "They learn, for

* See F. Wittels. *Die Befreiung des Kindes.* Hippocrates Verlag, Stuttgart, 1927, p. 77–78.

example, that other people's wishes are also real, and that if there are leaders there must be followers, in a way that no words of ours can teach them."*

In the nursery school this means that the person in charge is always present for the children's benefit, but that she interferes as little as possible in their lives, and above all that she avoids letting the "pressure" mentioned by Susan Isaacs become too noticeable. If so, the difficulties arising out of the brother and sister complex will tend to assert themselves and will thus have the chance to abate; at least they will be worked out rather than become more and more repressed. I am inclined to believe that many an incipient neurosis can thus be counteracted.

I mentioned in another context how Melanie Klein also emphasises that children bring their earlier conflicts into the new environment of the school. Though the following is concerned only with school life, the same applies to the nursery school: "School life also gives opportunity for a greater separation of hate and love than was possible in the small family circle. At school some children can be hated, or merely disliked, while others are loved. In this way, both the repressed emotions of love and hate—repressed because of the conflicts about hating a loved person—can find fuller expression in more or less socially accepted directions. Children ally themselves in various ways, and develop certain rules as to how far they can go in their expression of hatred or dislike of others. . . . Jealousy and rivalry for the teacher's love and appreciation, though they may be quite strong, are experienced in a setting different from that of home life. Teachers are, on the whole, further removed from the child's feelings, they bring

* S. Isaacs. *The Nursery Years.* 1942 Edition, p. 123.

less emotion into the situation than parents do, and they also divide their feelings among many children."*

Now we come to another matter worth attention in the nursery school. It has already been pointed out that the relations of brothers and sisters are in many cases disturbed by envy and this is expressed particularly frequently in the attitude of girls toward boys. I wish to return to this once more as it is certain to be observed in any nursery school run, in the usual way, on co-educational lines. Sex differences are often a problem even for the very young child. It can be assumed that a child who has grown up with brothers and sisters will know that a boy is different from a girl by the time he comes to a nursery school. In this case it will make no special impression when the children occasionally observe one another while undressing for games, bathing, or in the lavatory. The physical differences will not be noticed as strongly as by a child without brothers or sisters, though it should be remembered that a strange child may arouse more interest than a brother or sister, who are seen every day. One may also suppose in the case of single children that they have had opportunities to make observations in the street or on the playground, but presumably the more thorough observation that is possible in the nursery school may make a deeper impression. What should be the attitude of the nursery school teacher when she notices a child's marked attention, such as a puzzled look on his face, or surprised, embarrassed laughter? We must think about these matters and clarify our attitude to them. We know through psychoanalysis that the effect of suddenly seeing a thing and not understanding it may do lasting harm to children. When for example a boy notices the absence

* Melanie Klein and Joan Riviere. *Love, Hate and Reparation*, p. 95.

of the male organ in a girl, he may easily reach the conclusion that a previously existing organ has been taken
away or cut off. This explanation of an incomprehensible fact lies close at hand. On the other hand the little
girl is also amazed at the bodily differences, and frequently assumes (as psychoanalyses demonstrate again
and again) that something she once possessed has been
removed. In both cases the tendency exists to regard
the removal as a punishment for some wicked deed, very
frequently masturbation. Unconscious feelings of guilt
arise and the experience may contribute to make the
child anxious or make it feel inferior. The girl fears that
she has been harmed and the boy fears that the same
might happen to him. Hans Zulliger gives the following two good examples:* "A four-year-old boy stole
knives everywhere and nearly drove his parents to distraction. Analysis revealed that he feared that someone,
his father, would cut off his penis and make a girl of
him. This fear was relieved by the compulsion to steal
knives." "A girl who distinguished herself by tomboyish
behaviour (a real boy!) before puberty became ill from
profound depression. During analytical treatment it
was discovered that she had unconsciously hoped that
the missing organ would grow on and that she would
then be a boy. The depression showed her dissatisfaction with her sexual role."

The mental processes and emotional attitudes resulting from this have been summarised by Freud under
the heading of the "castration complex". (20) The
effect of this on the emotional development of a person
is of vital importance. In a girl the feeling of being less

---

* *Unbewusstes Seelenleben.* (The unconscious emotional life—the
main outlines of Freudian Psychoanalysis.) Stuttgart, Franksche
Verlagshandlung.

favoured and inadequate may easily develop as a result
of recognising that she is different. This feeling does not
necessarily have to become conscious, and its origin
is frequently not recognised. The so-called "masculinity
complex" (21) which will probably cause great difficulties
during the period of growth to womanhood may have
its starting point here. To reach the fulfilment of
her wish the girl will think a general approximation
to a boy's personality desirable for "she has seen
it, knows that she has not got it, and wants to have
it".*

Careful upbringing and thoughtful observation cannot
entirely nullify these influences, which are natural to a
certain degree. All the same, enlightened upbringing
will succeed in preventing excessive harm.

In some circumstances grave mistakes can be made in
the nursery school; on the other hand, an opportunity
is given there to remove some of the dangers of a trau-
matic experience of this kind. The child cannot be
spared the discovery of the physical differences between
the sexes; at some time and somehow the child is bound
to make this observation. So it is well not to insist on
too rigid a separation of the sexes. Undressing, bathing,
going to the lavatory—all these are to be taken as natural
and not worth attention. But one needs to be on one's
guard. If it appears that the children are observing
each other or if there are signs of astonishment over this
matter it is best to explain simply, that all boys are made
this way and all girls are made that way, and that this is
so from birth onwards. Psychoanalytical education
believes above all in behaving with complete frankness

---

* S. Freud. *Einige Psychischen Folgen des anatomischen Geschlechts-*
unterschieds. (Some psychological consequences of the anatomical
differences of the sexes.) Ges. Schriften, Bd. XI, p. 13.

towards the child. Secrecy concerning natural facts is regarded as harmful.

These questions are treated more fully in the next paragraph. Some hints to those in charge of nursery schools are given here first. A boy should never be threatened with mutilation of any kind—either of his ears in cases of disobedience, his hand if the child has been hitting someone, or his penis in order to prevent masturbation. It will be seen from the facts briefly indicated how such a threat may increase the castration complex. Girls should never be made to take second place. This frequently happens with female teachers who feel inferior as a result of their own complexes. The community life of the children must be based on equality and no differences must become apparent, unless they come from the children themselves. Games and tasks which exclude either the boys or the girls must not be used. For a long time the feminist movement has tried to suppress the old-fashioned educational theory of sex differentiation, partly because it is felt that justice should be done and partly in order to diminish the gulf between the sexes. We made the same efforts from another point of view the basis of which I have tried to describe. Turns of speech which one often still hears— "you are a boy, you must not play with dolls," or "a boy (a girl) doesn't do that", or "you are as scared as a girl" may be harmful to the community life of the children, to their attitude towards one another, and to their general psychological make-up. In most nursery schools equality of education and occupation is usually achieved except during free play, when dolls are often reserved for girls and horses for boys. But each child should be allowed to do what it feels inclined to do. We shall see later on that the child's freedom to play with what it likes is one of our principal requirements. It is wrong to assume that any special tendency in play, e.g., a boy playing with dolls, may conduce to a wrong type of development. Play activity springs from the emotions; no educational interference can ever touch the unconscious background of the urge to play, as it can do no more than try to control external manifestations. Play is merely an indication of what goes on in the child's emotions, and can never itself be the cause of psychological changes.

If we find in a child a strong desire to change its sex, we must give our attention to this. An increase of such an inclination may lead to faulty development, unless it is already a symptom of that. Observation of the child's entire behaviour must be our guide. If the symptom continues for long (in my experience it appears only for a short time) we must understand that it is a phenomenon which cannot be influenced by educational measures. It may happen that attempts to educate a child by teasing it or treating it contemptuously, or even, in the case of a boy, by an appeal to his masculine pride, will bring it to the point of concealing its real wishes. That these wishes will be effective all the same, indeed even more so in secret, seems to be proved by the frequent occurrence of the masculinity complex in women and similar disturbing influences in the sexual life of men. An approach will be found here by the psychoanalytical treatment. But as the following examples will show, such a wish in young children to be able to change sex more often than not appears only in a mild form and then disappears as it has come, without our having to interfere.

Of the many cases that revealed to me an increase and a subsequent decrease of discontent with one's own

49

sex, without any recognisable external reason, two may be cited here: (a) HENRY (aged 4) came to the nursery school "as a girl" one day. He wanted to be called ELSA, and became angry when we addressed him wrongly. His whole behaviour was that of a girl. This behaviour lasted for several days and then suddenly stopped, and in a 3-year period of observation never recurred. He became a real boy, very wild and getting on well with other boys. (b) MIRIAM wanted a boy's suit and a boy's bicycle for her fifth birthday. She said repeatedly that she wanted to be a boy, called herself FRITZE and conscientiously played only with boys in the nursery school. She showed great love towards a certain boy but treated him as if she was a boy as well. How strongly she had identified herself with her new role was shown by her counting herself as one of the boys when a roll call was taken. When this mistake was pointed out to her, she said quite seriously, "But I am not a girl". Her behaviour also altered after a few months and she seemed to forget her role as a boy. She became friendly with a girl in a typically feminine manner with much kissing, embraces and bouts of giggling. Two years later the seven-year-old has become "engaged" to a school friend and has exchanged rings with him, and the masculinity complex as far as it appeared in her conscious life seems to have been overcome. The solution of such conflicts by itself must not mislead us, of course, into treating more profound and lasting developments as harmless. These have been mentioned only to counteract the tendency to notice dangers too quickly. To return to children's play again and stress the possibility of other relationships, let us refer to HANNI, who played only with boys despite her doubtlessly quite feminine temperament. This was simply because she was loved and courted by them, and was therefore happier in their company, than in the company of girls who did not take so much notice of her.

Ambition, so frequently observed in children, especially girls in my experience, should be mentioned briefly. It manifests itself during nursery school occupations and can be connected with the child's attitude to its brothers and sisters. A younger sister often wants to be able to do everything her brother does. This caused ELLEN (aged 3) to protest vigorously against "being small". She did not want to come to the nursery school for days because she had been addressed as "little one" there, and the other children had treated her as the youngest. FRIEDA (4 years old) told me repeatedly that she could do this or that just as well as her brother. ELLEN climbed up a high ladder by the swing, although she was not free from fear, just to rival her brother. In such cases it is best to give ambition occasion to satisfy itself without making it greater by admiration or encouragement.

CHAPTER IV

FORMS OF THE
NURSERY SCHOOL CHILD'S EXPRESSION
OF HIS SEXUALITY

We now turn to the sexual interests of children, which any observer who is not herself sexually inhibited, can perceive again and again. The question "where children come from" arises frequently already at the nursery school age, unless free conversation has been barred by a strict régime.

In the nursery school we have mostly to deal with children who have been warped by a different up-bringing at home. We do know, however, that embarrassment begins to emerge after a certain age even without direct educational influence, and that this development is "organically determined and fixed by heredity".* In spite of this, my experience points to the stimulus of the children's domestic upbringing being an important contributing factor. FRITZ (aged 5) in my nursery school serves as proof. We were on very good terms and FRITZ spoke to me freely and openly of his problems. A rather unstable boy, he even gave way to changes of mood quite freely in my presence. At one time a powerful curiosity emerged in him. It made him examine everything, his attention being especially directed towards mechanical things—above all, the locks of doors and drawers. As other symptoms led me

* S. Freud. *Three Essays on the Theory of Sexuality.* Imago Publishing Co. London. 1949. p. 56.

to suppose that *another* urge lay behind *this* urge to acquire knowledge, that in fact FRITZ was pre-occupied with sexual problems, I tried to lead one of our conversations in this direction. As I asked him to tell me what was so much on his mind at the moment, and pointed out to him that he could say anything to me, as he knew, he said, agreeing with me: "Yes, but not such things." This reply confirmed my assumption only too clearly. FRITZ had recognised that certain subjects must not be discussed with grown-ups, and he therefore believed that I too would reject this topic.

Conversations among the children themselves are apt to contain the various "theories of birth" as psychoanalysis has made them know. What is remarkable is that the only child prefers to hold on to what he has thought out for himself or to what he has been told at home. Once I overheard a conversation in a next door room—which meant that the children could not include me in it—and I could not help observing that each of the children stuck to their own opinions irrespective of what the others said. The assumption is obvious that children in the midst of the Œdipus situation, are not particularly willing to recognise the falsehood of information which has been given them at home. Otherwise this peculiar and frequently observed trait would be difficult to understand, particularly in view of the ease with which they can normally be talked over in other matters. The conversation mentioned above ended with little ELSI crying angrily: "Anyhow at home the stork always brings our children!"

Now we must ask ourselves what our attitude to conversations of this nature should be, and how the child's urge for knowledge can be satisfied once it has been directed to this problem. In view of the different home influences to which the children are exposed, it is difficult to express a positive view. Many parents are still extraordinarily old-fashioned in their outlook, and there will frequently be trouble if the teacher, (as a psychoanalytically trained teacher would do as a matter of course) gives the child the information he desires. The question arises whether the nursery school, even in the interest of the child, is entitled to give sex education even against the parents' wishes. Each school must decide this question according to its own views and external circumstances. It also remains to be seen whether it is at all possible to alter the child's way of thinking once the direction has been set by parental influence. It goes without saying that picture books and fairy tales which mention the stork story and similar legends will not be used in the nursery school.

Above all, of course, it will be the task of the psychoanalytically trained teacher to win over the parents of nursery school children to our point of view at parent meetings and at interviews with individual fathers and mothers. Sex education of parents is sometimes more important than that of children. Only by rightly instructing the parents can we secure that freedom in relation to the child which is so desirable.

To summarise once again: we do not advocate the revelation of the facts concerning sex all at once, but rather a clear exposition of those questions the child asks about and in which he shows interest. It is a question of general openness, such as makes all attempts at secrecy superfluous and avoids the common halfhearted and over-romantic methods of sex education. *The aim is to guide the child in such a way that he learns to take all sexual matters for granted and as natural.* To make this possible the teacher must first of all rid herself of those prejudices and distorted attitudes which her own different education has most probably implanted in her. A close study of psychoanalytical literature,* or even better to have herself analysed, may be of help in this. We must suppose that in the course of reading, the acceptance of the findings offered will be made difficult by repressions and the results of inhibitions. Indeed many cases of the rejection of psychoanalysis may be traced to this.

Freud demonstrated for the first time that there is such a thing as the sexuality of the small child. Although Freud's discoveries were made a long time ago—the first treatise laying the foundation for future work, "Three Essays on the Theory of Sexuality" (*Drei Abhandlungen zur Sexualtheorie*) appeared in its first edition in 1904—they are still quietly ignored by most educators. It seems to me characteristic of the traditional attitude that the problem of the small child's sexuality is not discussed in present-day literature concerning nursery schools, that even in the writings of Maria Montessori† not one line is devoted to the child's sexuality, and finally that no observations on this have been made in nursery schools.

It would help if we understood why the symptoms of the child's sexuality are usually overlooked in the nursery school. This must be seen in relation to the general tendency not to see what one, perhaps uncon-

* In order to help those who have not the time to study Freud's writings, I have collected excerpts from them which deal with problems concerning the child. This collection appeared in 1951 under the name of *Freud zur Kinder-psychologie* in *Praxis der Kinder und Jugendpsychologie*, Herausgegeben v. Heinrich Meing, Verlag Hans Huber, Bern.

† At least not in her books published in Germany up to 1933.

sciously, does not wish to see. Is it not also remarkable that nothing is mentioned of the manifestations of sexuality in published diaries which deal with the development of small children? It is time that attention was paid to this so that mistakes made in educational method hitherto can be avoided in future.*

The only sign of the small child's sexuality which is usually recognised in nursery school circles and appreciated by them as an educational problem is masturbation. Masturbation and thumb-sucking have always been fought hard; the first as an indecent and unhealthy habit, the latter as "unseemly" for a "big" child of nursery school age. First we will make clear our attitude towards thumb-sucking, which is often observed in the nursery school, though not as frequently as masturbation. It is not, however, treated as a manifestation of a sexual instinct, as Freud treats it. I do not know what people are afraid of, when a child puts his thumb into his mouth to suck it with his tongue. What is commonly said is that the child's finger might get sore, or his teeth might not grow straight; but whatever other dangers are cited, they do not sound convincing and one may well wonder whether unconscious motives lie behind the fears of teachers and those in charge of children. Harm may occur only if there is an excess of thumb-sucking. Psychoanalytical experience has led me to the conclusion that thumb-sucking is a normal habit among very small children, and the slightly bigger

* Otto Fenichel, New York, writes in *The Psychoanalytic Study of the Child* (Imago Publishing Co. Ltd., London, 1945), p. 278: "If one remembers that prior to Freud science did not even know of the existence of infantile sexuality, one realises how intensely mankind must have wished that it actually did not exist. Awareness of this wish warns us against subscribing to the idea that infantile sexuality is dangerous, since this idea may be the product of the same tendency."

child need not be too severely restrained from doing it either.*

Why does a child suck? Well, as the result of an inner urge which guides him to this pleasurable activity. Observations show that the child's thumb-sucking is to be taken as a primitive manifestation of sexuality. Already by 1879 Lindner, a child specialist from Budapest, had pointed out the sexual nature of sucking.† The behaviour of the baby in arms when he is sucking, and the effects of this—partly causing excitement and partly acting as a sedative and soporific, forms the basis of these assumptions. It may just be this sexual note which has caused sucking to seem so worthy of attack in the eyes of educators. With most children the sucking habit stops by itself gradually, while with others it may last longer. Five- and six-year-olds, and here and there older ones, may be seen putting their fingers into their mouths when they are tired or sad. Thumb-sucking consoles. Why then conduct a campaign against it, when one must be fundamentally convinced of its futility and it only causes the child displeasure? A child tending to suck will either constantly relapse consciously when one is not present or will forget the prohibition again and again. A kindly upbringing which does not demand too many renunciations on the child's part counteracts thumb-

* Personal inquiries of dentists revealed that in cases of persistent thumb-sucking some effect on the teeth might be noticeable, but that this had not been observed very often. Opposed to this, however, is a pamphlet published by an association of dentists in Germany in 1925 for the enlightenment of parents, in which the alleged harmful effects of thumb-sucking were dramatically shown in words and pictures. But whether the method of weaning the child from thumb-sucking here advocated to the parents, which proposed practically sadistic measures, would do more psychological damage than the supposed physical effects of sucking, does not seem to have been considered by the author of the pamphlet and his advisers.

† *Jahrbuch fur Kinderheilkunde* N.F. XIV. Quoted by Freud.

sucking by indirect influence. Above all the child should be given much love and should be allowed to feel secure in it. This is of course important in the nursery school especially when a new child feels lonely and deserted in a new environment. Thus we can only underline Therese Simon's* recommendation, "to give such a child special attention and sympathy. A satisfactory occupation which distracts a dreamy, inactive child and one which he finds emotionally satisfying, may serve as an antidote. Thus the nursery school will be effective indirectly but should abstain from any punitive measures."

The same applies to masturbation. The motives which we assumed to be behind the campaign against thumb-sucking seem to apply to an even greater degree in the case of masturbation. Psychoanalysis demonstrates that masturbation should be understood as natural in this age group. Normally it does no harm and does not need further observation. Only in cases where excessive masturbation is noticeable should we ask ourselves whether this should not be countered by psychoanalytical measures so that the child does not fixate on the habit. It should also be said here that frequently a change takes place by itself and that after masturbation has reached a climax abatement may take place. After this, substitutive gratification can frequently be observed. Thus I once saw the temporary appearance of another habit in the case of a six-year-old girl with whom excessive masturbation had begun to abate during psychoanalytical treatment. ERNA constantly put something into her mouth—mostly the corner of her apron, and sucked it. Gradually this also ceased. Paper chewing, eating sand, playing with the cuticle and nail biting are usually substitutive gratifications when masturbation

* Therese Simon, *Das Doppelleben des Kindes*, p. 82.

has been broken off too abruptly often because of severe prohibitions and threats.

We should never use the dangerous method of trying to rid a child of any habit by playing on its fears. In its after-effects the threat itself is much more harmful than the supposed evil. Many neuroses in later life can be traced back to threats that caused fear in childhood. Those who attempt to rid the child of a habit by force forget the basic rule of all modern treatment: forbearance by proceeding *gradually*. No treatment of grown-ups is ever carried through with such violence as is supposed suitable for powerless and emotionally vulnerable children. The damages resulting from this, and the danger to the good relations between educator and child, need no further emphasis.

The danger of imitation in the nursery school is obvious but need not be worried about too much. Freud shows that the awakening of a child's sexuality may happen spontaneously from inner causes without seduction having taken place—although Freud does not entirely deny the possibility of the influence of imitation.* As long as a child does not masturbate openly, that is, in a manner which makes him noticeable to other children, no notice should be taken of it. If, for the sake of other children, interference is essential, this should take the form of a friendly talk. If the relationship with the person in charge is a good one, such a conversation will sometimes work. Whether this is in the child's interest still remains an open question. The struggle to break the habit even when undertaken in such a case out of love, for the sake of a loved person, may exceed the child's power and may lead to depressing guilt feelings each time the attempt fails.

* Freud. *Three Essays on the Theory of Sexuality.* p. 68, 69.

Psychology in the Nursery School

From my own experiences I would like to emphasise that children do not seem to take notice of secret masturbation (shifting to and fro on a chair, or pressing themselves against tables) or at any rate do not react to it by imitation. What I have noticed frequently and believe to be a fairly widespread phenomenon characteristic of this age group, is that children try to handle each other in their games (e.g., playing doctor). As one cannot know whether the passive child may not be receiving a violent stimulus for the first time, the effects of which in individual cases we cannot foresee, we should do well to discourage such games, in the interest of the child's adjustment to reality also. This should not be done by energetic measures or by making a fuss about it, but by distraction, and, as in the case of masturbation, a talk about it.*

Some light should be thrown on another sexual pleasure of the child, which is usually not included in this field, but is considered a form of sexuality by Freud. We are dealing with the pleasure stimuli in relation to the anal (22) area. In the nursery school we have occasion to observe in many children an open rejoicing in filth, and an inclination to use words connected with the process of elimination and swearwords as well. According to psychoanalysis, the interest in dirt and the use of forbidden words are remains, and to a certain extent substitutes for the dirtiness of the babe in arms, his tendency to smear himself with fæces.

Here are a few observations. THEO (aged 4) noticed a dog's excrement by a tree while on a walk one day. He pointed to it, pleased and interested, and finally danced round the tree repeatedly calling out "a-a". On this

* "Onanie" *Zeitschrift für Psychoanalytische Pedagogik. Special Magazine Edition.* II Heft 4–6. 1928.

day his dance of joy was repeated at every tree where he could discover dog's excrement. RITA (aged 5) refused to sit on the floor while doing gymnastics. Mindful of her mother's warnings she explained "that's not allowed, it's dirty there". After a few moments, "I'll do it all the same," and she continued, beaming all over her face, "isn't it lovely?" ANNIE (aged 4) was very fond of peeping through gaps in the wall of a rural privy while it was being used, because she wasn't let in. GERDA (aged 3) went into the same privy with the greatest of pleasure, lifted up the wooden cover, looked down and deeply inhaled the smell. As FRED (aged 3) had been told at home that he was not to use any bad words in the nursery school, he went up to his grandmother before leaving home and whispered all the words then used by him into her ear. Then he said satisfied, "now I don't have to swear in the nursery school any more". The same boy had the peculiar habit of saying of anything that pleased him, that it stank. As his mother had drawn my attention to this, I was not surprised when he happily cried out, while having his morning milk, "This stinks!"

Now comes the question of how the love of dirt is to be dealt with by education in view of these associations. These examples of the manifestations of the love of dirt leave no doubt that it is not just a form of "naughtiness". The best attitude will be to pay the least possible attention to these things. Prohibitions stimulate and only lead to furtiveness. At home the use of words connected with anal matters was strictly prohibited to PETER (aged 5) who then took his chance in the nursery school, withdrew into a corner and did nothing but repeat to himself with visible enjoyment the words forbidden to him at home. Here, as well as with much other behaviour of children, we must assume that a great deal will pass off on its own and through the influence of environment. Thus we can watch such symptoms of a child's instinctual urge without undue worry. In any case we think it advisable to give the child in free conversation the opportunity to liberate those of his wishes and thoughts that defy repression.

Of course it must not be forgotten that the use of undesirable words can arise like an epidemic in a nursery school and this, apart from other disadvantages, entails parental censure. I have known weeks to pass with hardly any anal terms being used. If then a child enters a period of increased interest in anal matters and this is revealed to the other children, for example in his painting and modelling, we shall find almost the whole group infected before long. Nothing had been put into the children's minds that was not already there before, only an interest that had been dormant had been awakened. I regard as proof the fact that some children, even though not overtrained by upbringing, take no part in the reaction described, and the anal interest of the others strikes no chord with them.

Thus it is well not to attach too much importance even to the external manifestations of this matter, but to observe the expressions of children as symptomatic for individuals. Every opportunity should be used to create new channels for their interests (sublimation), by finding the child suitable occupations. At any rate it should be obvious that we ought to be most sparing with our prohibitions. *Repression instead of sublimation, and the possibility of reaction therefrom lead to a fixation of the interest in the unconscious.*

CHAPTER V

EROTICALLY TINGED FRIENDSHIPS
IN EARLY CHILDHOOD

Behaviour arising out of a child's sexual instinctual force shows itself in friendships with erotic tendencies such as I have sometimes observed beginning in the nursery school. To me such friendships seem important enough to merit the attention of the educator, as I gained the impression that the cases I observed were not isolated cases but instances of a more general nature. Out of them arose problems which may be of importance both in their psychological and educational implications.

I made inquiries whether similar observations had been made in other places and what importance had been attached to them there. Queries in educational circles and among parents did not produce any useful material, but I noticed that here and there strong friendships had been noticed, without any special attention being paid to them. Naturally the erotic implications of these friendships are not usually recognised. As I have said before, in general the tendency exists not to notice what one does not wish to notice.*

Most probably the "harmless friendships" did not appear important enough to merit closer attention.

* I have noticed in myself before my own psychoanalysis that I did not observe these types of friendship despite years of work in the educational field. The opponents of psychoanalysis tend to give as a reason for this fact that psychoanalytically orientated teachers see things in children that they *wish* to see. As proof against this it may suffice that I have no more material than is presented here, although I paid special attention to the problem.

Psychology in the Nursery School

Parents, who sense the erotic basis of such relationships, without admitting it to themselves, tend to guard themselves against this unwelcome recognition by teasing and jokes, in short by not taking it seriously. On one occasion I found the relatives of a child that was in love frightened by his behaviour. They thought it a perverse inclination or an unhealthy early development and were helpless faced with this fact. In such cases a talk with the parents enlightening them will calm them, and be in the child's interest.

I will now give the material collected in my nursery school:

1st Case. STEFFI (5 years old)* was the focal point of the nursery. Although the girl did not seem particularly attractive to grown-ups she was like a magnet to all the boys. Whatever occupations she chose, they were also taken up by the boys. STEFFI did not seem particularly conscious of her influence, at any rate she did not use it for her own advantage. WILLIAM (aged 4) was specially in love with STEFFI. He disclosed his all-absorbing love on the following occasion. One day he came to the nursery school beaming all over his face and told me straight away that he was going to the bank during the lunch hour. Although he did not produce a more detailed explanation, it was obvious by his behaviour that the walk to the bank meant something extraordinary and beautiful to him. Then he told me: "Father is sending me a cheque at lunchtime, and with it I am to go to the bank and buy myself my STEFFI." The boy had taken his father's teasing seriously. The prospect of absolute ownership most probably made him

* The ages given here are those at the time during which the events mainly happened; sometimes the developments lasted over a longer period of time.

happy. When his mother came to the nursery school without a cheque during the lunch hour, WILLIAM eased his feelings first by weeping bitterly and then by a tantrum.

2nd Case. PETER (aged 5) was a particularly intelligent boy, sure of himself, with a confident manner. He ceased to be eminent as a self-sufficient personality in the nursery school when PAUL (5 years) got him to be his friend. The two withdrew from all the others to play only by themselves—if possible in a corner—where they could not be seen, PAUL trying to get PETER to take part in games that led to masturbation.

3rd Case. KARL and FRITZ (both 5 years old) were close friends. When together, also outside the nursery school, they always seemed noisy, over-excited, rumbustious and silly. By the excitement emanating from them they were a disturbing influence on the rest of the group. His friendship with FRITZ was of special importance to KARL. All the other children refused to have any dealings with him, and brusquely rejected his frequently renewed attempts to approach them. Thus KARL revived in the presence of FRITZ by whom he felt himself wanted. Of course this increased KARL'S suffering, when FRITZ, as happened occasionally, did not want to play with him, took no notice of him, and went to other children. At such times KARL was quite unstable, bad-tempered, noisy, unpleasant and rude to all the other children. An attempt was made to lessen their growing excitement by separating the boys. They came to the nursery school on different days now. FRITZ joined the other children without further ado, grew calmer and did not seem to miss KARL. The latter asked for his friend once or twice and regretted that he was not coming. He occupied himself intensively by himself, seemed happy, and succeeded sometimes in making contact with the other children. His over-excitement did not show itself any longer.

4th Case. MIA (aged 5) at first loved TOM (aged 4); for her the nursery school meant being together with him. At home she talked of him a great deal and her mind seemed completely preoccupied with him. As she wanted to be a boy and was completely absorbed in playing this part, she deliberately played only boys' games with TOM. She behaved to him like a boy and was somewhat domineering towards him. TOM played a fairly passive part but seemed to love her quietly and was less moody than usual in her company. (He was suffering from jealousy of a newly-born brother.) When TOM left off coming to the nursery school and MIA did not find him present when she returned from her summer holidays, she did not seem to miss him. She soon formed a friendship with LENI (aged 6), almost as intense as that with TOM. Her role as a boy seemed forgotten during this time, although they mostly played boys' games, i.e., ships and policemen.

5th Case. ERNA (aged 6) began to court ERICH (aged 6) intensively, and after a time was able to win over this rather reticent tough boy. They always sat together, decided to get married later on and talked of the wedding, but soon the attachment died down. After that ERNA only really played with girls in the nursery school, but as soon as the elder brother of a child there came for a visit, she no longer took notice of anything around her, flirted with him, sat close to him, if possible on his lap, and no child, not even his sister, was permitted to have anything to do with him. On such a day none of the usual attractions of the nursery school existed for her.

6th Case. GUENTHER (4 to 6 years old) had a friend LORE of about his own age outside the nursery school.

Erotically Tinged Friendships

She absolutely dominated him and he was quite devoted to her. Though not at all modest usually, he felt himself to be small and insignificant by her side. She was able to do what she wanted with him. Her mother heard the following in the next room, repeated several times by LORE: "The end bit must come off, what is it there for anyhow?" The mother on entering saw that LORE was cutting off strands of the boy's hair. This action must be understood symbolically (23). GUENTHER'S passive behaviour showed that he was sacrificing his masculinity for the sake of his love.

Once when GUENTHER'S mother was unfriendly to LORE, he made a great demonstration of his tenderness towards the latter, although he usually tended to be rather brusque in his friendship.

GUENTHER was happy when he was allowed to bring his friend to the nursery school as a visitor. This was *his* home and he was sure of himself, she however was a stranger and ill-at-ease. Here he was visibly her superior and this brought out in him the self-confidence that was suppressed by her.

LORE became an influence against the nursery school. One day GUENTHER did not want to come to the nursery school any longer. It appeared that LORE had called the nursery school "daft" and had asked him whether he would not rather stay with her.

It seemed probable to me that there was a connection between GUENTHER'S difficulties in becoming adjusted to the nursery school and LORE. GUENTHER made no contact with the other children because the focal point of his emotions, LORE, was outside the nursery school. Only after about two years did he become friendly with another boy, and apart from that began to play with most of the other children. This was at a time when

67

the friendship with LORE had dissolved because of external reasons.

7th Case. INGE and KURT (both 3 years old) loved each other and would only play together, asked for each other as soon as they arrived in the morning, and seemed to be only really happy when they were together. The more intelligent INGE was the dominating influence. Both children were very tender to each other, and whenever they met on the corridor kissed each other in passing.

8th Case. Like KARL and FRITZ (*Case* 3) ROLF and GERHARD (aged 4) stimulated each other. They behaved to each other with a tenderness I have never observed before. ROLF usually took the initiative and GERHARD accepted it gladly. Their need for affection was so great that they would suddenly fall into each other's arms, hold each other close and kiss while in the street, playing or eating, and would only part with great reluctance. I have never noticed that there was any connection between a game and such an outbreak of tenderness. Neither boy paid any attention to the communal attractions of the nursery school; they ignored all suggestions that they should occupy themselves with the materials and games at hand, and were only intent on playing with each other. In a sense they took refuge in their play in order to belong to each other and to be close together in it, and if possible to be in a room without the other children being present. It struck me that GERHARD (gladly it seemed) went to the occupational toys and worked with them in a concentrated manner as soon as ROLF was absent. But the moment ROLF came, he stopped in order to play with his friend. ROLF, on the other hand, did not occupy himself at all when his friend was absent. Apart from the usual boys' games, playing at being a surgeon came into the foreground after ROLF had had his tonsils removed. Other children were also asked to join in this game, but ROLF was always the doctor. Then the "little dwarf game" made its appearance. It had been proposed by ROLF, was to be played only by the two of them and was to be kept secret. I was refused an explanation of the game when I asked for it. Later I found that the "little dwarf game" consisted of ROLF's unbuttoning GERHARD's trousers and masturbation.

The following conversation between GERHARD and another boy seemed to show that his relations with ROLF were beginning to be a nuisance to him. When the other boy asked him to play with him (ROLF had not arrived) GERHARD gladly agreed to do so, but then said thoughtfully, and it seemed to me moodily, "but when my friend comes, I won't be able to". Then he added, giving a sigh of relief, "but perhaps he isn't coming". When I interposed that ROLF would come as it was his day here, GERHARD added in a hopeful tone, "well, perhaps he is ill!"

When ROLF soon after this stopped coming to the nursery school, GERHARD was in a bad mood for a day, but then joined the other children and was able to occupy himself alone satisfactorily as well. He did not inquire after ROLF. The latter asked everyone in the nursery school he met "what is my friend doing?" It might be emphasised here that the term "friend" is not usually used at this early age, but was a term used with obvious pleasure by ROLF.

9th Case. HANNI (aged 5) seemed very sure of herself from the first day she came, took everything as a matter of course, participated in all activities, but never showed any sign of excitement. She was the same with boys— outwardly she was always cool and on her part nothing that was erotically tinged was to be noticed in her relationships with boys. Besides it should be pointed out

69

that although HANNI was on good terms with all the girls, nothing in the way of a friendship or a visit to their homes ever occurred. Even when HELEN, who was related to her and of whom she was otherwise apparently very fond, came to the nursery school, she did not bother with her. HANNI's first friend was BOB (aged 5). He dominated all other children and liked also to appear bossy towards grown-ups. He rejected all rules and resisted strongly whenever we wanted anything from him. Towards HANNI he was absolutely obedient, however, and adjusted himself to her in every respect. In contrast to his tone to other children (e.g., "go away you damned dogs!") he was never rude or violent to her. He remained unchanged towards HANNI even on his nervous violent days. I only heard him threaten her with a beating once, when she would not play with him alone, for occasionally they allowed one other child to play with them. This was the only cause for quarrelling between them, as according to their moods one or the other tended to be jealous. I chanced to hear the following conversation. BOB to HANNI: "Are you playing with us? ELSA is also playing." HANNI: "Then I'm not going to play with you." BOB: "And if ELSA does not play with us?" HANNI: "Then I will play with you." BOB: "But when you are away on your summer holidays, can I play with ELSA then?" HANNI: "Yes, but only then—not as long as I am here". BOB and HANNI played "family" on many occasions. This included cooking, going out together and sleeping. Frequently they also constructed a ship that was used as a house after it had been built. Often the two conversed in baby language.

After his return from a holiday BOB became jealous of HORST, who had in the meantime emerged as HANNI's

70

friend. He got rid of his anger on all of us and was restless and silly, but towards HANNI and HORST, with whom he made friends, he behaved quite equitably.

HORST seemed more in love outwardly and was more tender and delicate in his demonstrations of love. He lacked the desire to dominate. Frequently one might observe him secretly stroking or kissing her hand (a demonstration of affection usual with him towards people he loved). He seemed happy whenever he saw HANNI and very openly also transferred his love to HANNI's mother, whom he finally called "mummy" (he said "mama" to his own mother). Whenever he was not together with HANNI he talked of her a great deal. At night he used to masturbate in bed for a long time, shaking his bed, and while doing this he talked to himself loudly. The nursery school and HANNI formed the content of his soliloquies.

While HANNI was absent from the nursery school he did not want to come either. When she had a sore throat, he too complained of pains in his throat. It remained an open question whether he was identifying himself with her or whether it was an excuse not to have to come to the nursery school.

HORST protected HANNI and helped her when it seemed necessary to him. Once a piece of grit had blown into HANNI's eye and he came to me and said sadly: "HANNI's eye is hurting *such* a lot"—though HANNI denied this. HORST said devotedly, anxious to perform a love service: "If I had a big bandage I would tie it over her eye." When a boy expressed the intention of cutting off the heads of all children, HORST thought that this could never happen, for HANNI's sake: he, of course, could defend himself, but HANNI couldn't.

Once a boy had thrown sand at HANNI, and at BOB's

71

and Horst's instigation a regular conspiracy broke out against him, which upset the nursery school for several days. Peace was only restored after the offender had asked Hanni's pardon.

Guenther's (see Case 6) love for Hanni had so far never come into the open. But when his mother told him one day that Hanni was visiting him in the afternoon, he blushed deeply and fell round her neck with joy.

10*th Case.* Michael (aged 6 to 9). Although Michael was older than the age group I usually observed, I do not want to omit his case, as it seems to show specially characteristic signs; also the girls involved were still in the nursery school stage. For external reasons Michael continued to visit the nursery school occasionally until he was nine years old.

Michael had been in the country during the summer. When he returned he whispered into my ear: "Do you know what I would like to do most? When I return to X, I want to give Lotte a kiss!"

First of all Michael fell in love with Grete (aged 5) in the nursery school. He became her protector, took her home, and seemed happy when permitted to visit her in the afternoon. After Grete left, the friendship continued for a long time outside the nursery school. Next it was the turn of the four-year-old Else. He tried to spoil her and to make her happy by all sorts of devices. For example he brought along his toy-motor car "for all the children" as he said, but really the only thing of importance was to drive Else home from the nursery school. On both sides the relationship was tender and restrained. Michael behaved most graciously towards Else's mother, and in the end transferred a great deal of his affection to her.

Both Grete and Else accepted Michael's adoration

Erotically Tinged Friendships

quite calmly, but were not especially keen on him and were not at all excited by it.

After Else left, Anni (aged 5) followed. She absolutely rejected Michael and never wanted to play with him—and so a proper courtship began on his part. Whatever he said or did was meant for her; his voice and gestures always revealed if what he said to me or others was really meant for her. When he had noticed Anni's rejection, his voice grew shrill with excitement. Jealousy was visibly plaguing him. He constantly observed the girl and had a tortured look on his face whenever she spoke a friendly word to someone else. Occasionally Anni was a little less frigid, which was noticed by Michael and I was told: "To-day she is a little nicer". The fact that the boy was conscious of the whole situation made it worse. His inner excitement took a frightening form and his facial expression revealed what went on within him. Otherwise a most obedient boy who had transferred his affection to me, he became so cheeky to me, that I was at a loss to know what would happen next. He was so touchy and irritable towards the other children that they all turned against him. The more Anni tortured him by obviously ignoring him, the more he took his revenge on the others.

When Michael went to his elementary school, this unpleasant situation came to an end. But as both children lived in the same street, I knew that Michael's suffering would continue. After three months he visited me, and among the first things he told me was: "I am quite finished with Anni now. She put out her tongue to me in the street." I had the feeling that this end had brought him relief.

The erotic element in the friendships here described

73

can be summed up as follows. The children lived predominantly with and through their friends (only partly in the nursery school, and partly outside it). "The emotional focal point was shifted from the individual to his opposite" (Hans Reichard). The children sought to be alone with each other, withdrew themselves from the group and made up their fantasies (plays) together. They sought physical contact, exchanged tenderness and some tried masturbation games. Strong jealousy, the struggle to be sole possessor, domination on one side and submission up to complete slavery on the other, active and passive behaviour of each partner emerged clearly. The similarity of the development of these relations to those of adults was remarkable.

The most important difference is only how quickly the relationship is forgotten or got over when a separation occurs, at least as far as one can infer from noticeable signs. It requires further investigation whether there are stronger reactions which would only be discovered with the aid of analysis. It does, however, seem possible to me that here too the child has a stronger repressive mechanism at his disposal than the grown-up, and that with its help he is better able to overcome the anguish at being separated.*

* To illustrate my point I will quote a few brief remarks from Dorothy Burlingham and Anna Freud's book *Infants without Families, The Case for and against residential nurseries* (Allen & Unwin, Ltd., London, 1943.) (They are thinking of normal conditions as opposed to residential homes for children.) "Friendships of long duration are believed to be very rare among young children. Lasting attachments are formed to grown-ups or to older children; playmates of the same age are used for play only, and friendships fall apart when the momentary reason for them (the play) has ended." op. cit., p. 39. The following examples show behaviour between infants which is hardly different from the expression of love and affection between adults, p. 41-42. One morning RALPH was looking at a story book, pointed excitedly to the capital B on the right page and called out: "Look, look, that's HENRY and me!" The form of the letter B suggested to him the picture of two friends embracing each other, (p. 42).

Erotically Tinged Friendships

As I have purposely reported the cases observed without giving my own point of view as an educator, the questions arising from them will now be dealt with briefly. The most important point will be to inquire to what extent if at all these friendships of children are capable of influencing the later sexual life and the formation of character, and whether they can underlie the development of neuroses; all this in view of the material obtained from the psychoanalyses of grown-ups. It seems certain to me that the violence of the expression of emotions and the general reaction to friendship, have frequently to be regarded as neurotic symptoms. Further light should be thrown on the question whether homosexual relations have lasting effects in this direction or whether they are to be evaluated only as a transitional stage. While we can see the after effects of the Œdipus-situation in children of this age-group who have formed homosexual attachments, it must be remembered that one of the partners is usually seduced and that for him it must be a first experience.* Deeper research is needed to find out how strong the effects are of disappointment, unrequited affection, tortures of jealousy and on the other hand too easily gained successes; nor do we know the influence of the reaction of the group toward an individual child (attraction and rejection). Psychoanalysis has discovered the fact that early experiences have the most far-reaching effects, and in recognition of this, it must not be doubted that the events described here can have great importance although they seem outwardly so transient.

A point of view regarding the education of children can only be founded on a deeper examination of the questions arising out of the psychological material here.

* S. Freud. *Three Essays on the Theory of Sexuality.* p. 68.

75

Psychology in the Nursery School

It is useless and in my opinion presumptuous to interfere or to try to present a new viewpoint in some way
unless we know more about the factors involved. It is
furthermore questionable whether educational measures
are at all feasible, and under what conditions they are
desirable. At any rate it seems to me, after my own
experiences, that interference with a child, while he is
under the influence of an erotic friendship, is rarely
successful. The partner in the friendship exercises a
greater influence than the educator. It would be valuable
to establish whether the friendships of children in this
age-group should not be seen as substitutive satisfactions, arising out of an unsatisfactory Œdipus situation.* It is quite possible that there are already clear
instances of transferred love; the cases observed by me
took place mostly at an age when the Œdipus Complex
was diminishing. Of the twenty-four children mentioned
two were 3 years old, four 4 years, fifteen 5 years, two
6 years and one more than 6 years old. (Eighteen were
only children, two born late, and four children with
brothers and sisters.) It is impossible to assess with my
material to what extent the loneliness of only children
has an effect on the formation of such friendships. In
the group of children observed by me, the only children
used to predominate by about two-thirds; further observation of differently composed groups would first be
necessary.

* In a discussion of this subject on the basis of material supplied
by me, the idea was expressed that it was perhaps one of the functions
of the nursery school to give the child an opportunity to form erotic
friendships.

CHAPTER VI

THE RUNNING OF THE NURSERY SCHOOL

I summarise once more what the nursery school has to offer the child. We have learnt of the need to loosen family ties when they are excessively close, and discovered the advantages of living together with other children and making the child's adjustment to reality easier by introducing him into a larger group. It has been indicated that it is the task of the nursery school to afford the child opportunities for sublimation, and substitutive satisfactions for instinctual renunciation. Now the question is how the nursery school is to be run in order to achieve these aims.

We have to place the child in the community (which, with Froebel, we shall regard as an enlarged family) and to give him an opportunity to lead a life, suited to childhood as such and to him individually. First it should be explained how we endeavour to make the adjustment to reality easier, by recognising that the small child is a pleasure-ego (24) (Freud) from whom a renunciation should only be demanded if a substitutive satisfaction is provided in exchange.

It has already been remarked that the process of being educated is made easier for the child within a group, because there he does not feel himself to be the solitary suffering party. In this sense the visit to the nursery school helps the child to adjust himself to the demands of the community. The renunciations the child has to make to this end, or rather in this instance to adjust

77

himself to the nursery school, must be compensated for by other values. In Froebel's opinion "the aim of the nursery school is to bring joy", and in expressing that thought we have already taken a step forward. As long as grown-ups do not interfere with and correct the children too strictly, a harmonious atmosphere will grow by itself out of the business of living and playing together, though some of the children's family conflicts may be transferred. It is not necessary for the person in charge to try creating a pleasurable atmosphere artificially by means of games and occupations, as was done in nursery schools conducted on the old plan. Children amuse themselves simply by being together, so long as they are given the means to occupy themselves and the freedom necessary for play, movement and creativeness, and—for those who want or need it—opportunities for separation from the group.

All the same we know that the life of the community demands much of the child and that there are many things which for the sake of others he must not do. He must be considerate, must use caution, and even in a free nursery school he must not give expression to his own wishes, instinctual demands, and affects without restraint. This restraint on the child arising out of community life is part of the value of the nursery school. For it sets the child's feet on the path he must take in later life in any case; but it does so, assuming the nursery school is conducted correctly, gently and in a manner which causes the child relatively little inconvenience. If we wished to spare the child all renunciations he would remain static at his present stage of development. He can and will only grow up through restrictions.

In this connection it is important to emphasise that according to the experience of child psychologists too

78

The Running of the Nursery School

indulgent an upbringing gives a child insufficient support. The small child wants to be able to rely on grown-ups close to him and counts on their help in his fight against the aggressive instincts dominating him. Susan Isaacs writes on this: "He needs to feel that they (mother or nurse) will not let him bite or kick or hurt them, nor spoil, dirty or break up everything. He needs to know that they love him in spite of his faults and angers, and that they will not revenge themselves upon him by severe punishments. Mere indulgence, however, is no help. The child seeks control from the outside just because he has yet so little control of himself, and becomes so afraid of his jealousy and anger and destructive wishes, unless he is sustained against them by the grown-up's decision."*

Torsten Ramer (Child Guidance Clinic, Stockholm) also remarked in a lecture that the absolutely free upbringing of a child may have disadvantages. "Too much freedom in upbringing for normal children means that the child has no one against whom to pit his forces. This means that the child receives too little support during his growing-up."†

A further view is that of Frederick H. Allen, Child Guidance Clinic, Philadelphia: "Without some frustration there could be no awakening of the will to assert and to test our capacity to deal with external forces."‡

These authors are quoted here to show that some change has taken place in the theories of psychologically orientated education. While psychoanalytical educa-

---

* *Childhood and After. Some Essays and Clinical Studies.* Routledge & Kegan Paul, Ltd., London, 1948, p. 63.

† Lecture "Aggression in relation to Family Life", op. cit.

‡ Lecture "Aggression in relation to Emotional Development, Normal and Pathological". Int. Conference on Child Psychiatry, London, August, 1948.

79

tional theory at first exaggerated the concept of free education and all prohibitions or restrictions were considered harmful by some, it has been learnt, as we see, that absolute freedom cannot be considered desirable. It does seem obvious however that the *form* of interference is of the greatest importance. Thus we agree with Anna Freud's view that attempts to hold down manifestations of the child's increasing aggressiveness, i.e., the use of counter-aggressiveness by the grown-up, are unsuccessful.*

In order to avoid misunderstandings let it be repeated again that we recognise the necessity of the small child having to bear a certain amount of unpleasure, but we ease it with the means available in the nursery school environment. Artificial, so-called educational, prohibitions we reject, since the demands arising out of the community are in themselves great. The grown-up "urge to educate" to use Wilhelm Reich's expression, is, however, a danger which threatens children. It is certain that where restrictions on freedom, and other types of prohibition and correction of the child's behaviour exceed a certain measure, where the child is continually being nagged because of this urge to educate, there opposition will result instead of adjustment, and with it more obstacles to the adjustment to reality.

As mentioned before, the psychoanalytically-minded teacher will have quite a different conception of the child's adjustability from that usually found in other circles. We tend to limit, if not reject entirely, the cocept of the "good" child. In some cases it will even be the task of the nursery school to encourage a child to be

* Lecture "Aggression in relation to Emotional Development, Normal and Pathological". International Conference on Child Psychiatry London, August, 1948.

The Running of the Nursery School

"naughtier", that is, to rid him of the good behaviour created by inhibitions or strict upbringing and to help him to be freer. In short, to take himself more for granted and to lessen the demands on his unconscious ego-ideal. Why we consider this desirable need not be explained again. Here besides the sphere of influence created by us, the nursery school itself, that is the presence of other children, will play an important part. If we agree with Reik's view* that the community is a means of lessening guilt feelings, one should be able to assume, as we have often experienced, that children are more daring in their "naughtiness" in the company of others. They allow themselves wider scope and occasionally do things which they know to be prohibited or indecent just because their guilt feelings are pacified by the thought: I am not doing it on my own, the others don't think it's awful either.

Now we have reached a point that deserves serious attention. We saw that we must expect a child to adapt himself, and yet we take steps to restrict his good behaviour. It needs emphasising that the happy mean is not easily found and it will need tact on the part of the teacher to find a way that does not end in chaos and yet does justice to the individual child. We must realise that this manner of exercising authority is very much more difficult than the authoritative method of leadership practised formerly (and in many cases still to-day). In the same way I have had to recognise that in practice the outward passivity of the person in charge, demanded by Montessori, is considerably more difficult than the more active manner practised in the older sort of nursery school. It is, of course, so much easier to prescribe, to

* T. Reik, *Geständniszwang und Strafbedürfniss.* International P.S.A. Verlag, Vienna, 1925. p. 20.

order, to be the giver and directly the leader, than merely to be present, observing and awaiting developments. Everything in him drives the teacher to interfere, to improve, and to instruct; indeed she would not have become a teacher at all had not the make-up of her emotional life urged her to this sort of activity. Yet we recognise as Maria Montessori's most important achievement the fact that she has given children better opportunities to develop by insisting on the person in charge adopting a passive role. The psychoanalytically-minded teacher agrees with Montessori in also advocating the independence of the child, from his own point of view. We recognise independence as a healthy basis for the development of the ego. The disadvantages of retaining the child on an infantile level of development by spoiling him have been pointed out and should again be considered in this connection. In getting used to being independent I see one way of freeing the child from the oppressive power grown-ups have over him. In view of the feelings of inferiority and guilt that arise so easily, and are mostly in existence by the time the nursery school age has been reached, being created or increased because of the oppression and spoon-feeding so customary in the usual education, we must insist that the child and his own endeavours be taken seriously. In no way must the child come to consider himself a creature on a level beneath us. He must move freely, establish himself in freedom, and freely work for what he needs in his development. If the concept of adjustment to reality is understood as "mastering life with as little suffering as possible" it is clear that self-possession, security and self-confidence, and the lessening of the child's guilt feelings, must be the aim of all education. Perhaps this theoretical view is best supported by this information from a children's home; Vera Schmidt reports: "According to our experience, adjustment to reality succeeds most easily with children who are self-confident and independent. Thus the way to adjustment would be found by increasing self-confidence."*

The demand for strong independence and self-education does not rule out the subordination of the child in the nursery school to a leading personality—as a mother substitute. On to her the child must be able to transfer the positive and negative emotions he brings with him from his family. If severance from too close a tie with the family is to be one of the tasks of the nursery school, the substitutive satisfactions offered by us must certainly create an equilibrium. The child's need for love, his anxious search for support and security, his need for consolation if he feels deserted by his mother in the nursery school, must find such reactions in the teacher as will lead the child to continue there the emotional attitudes he has so far felt only towards his parents. Children spoilt with love must not at once suffer too many deprivations in their new surroundings; and those who at home felt a lack of love should find with us warmth of feeling and greater opportunities for love. This is what is new, and perhaps the most important contribution of psychoanalysis to education: the effort, by consciously regulating the circumstances of the child's transference, to make the relationship of the child with his teacher serve a useful purpose in the child's education. The child ought to make sacrifices and adjust himself out of love for his teacher, that is voluntarily. We should, therefore, try to direct the child's love to-

* Vera Schmidt, *Psychoanalytische Erziehung in Sowjetrussland.* Bericht ueber das Kinderheim Laboratorium in Moskau. Int. P.S.A. Verlag 1924. p. 16.

wards us, and this should not be left to chance, but by our own conduct towards the child the transference should be achieved as quickly as possible. The child's love of the person in charge will thus become the pivot of our educational efforts, which, let it be underlined again, should not be a coercive activity. We are there only as focal points towards whom the child strives, whose attention he desires, and whom he wants to emulate. In this care must be taken not to appear too superior, so that the child loses heart and we seem unapproachable. A feeling of fellowship does not exclude leadership but relieves it of some of its oppressiveness. As we reject punishment in the nursery school, the only regulating factor will be our behaviour to the child, our joy at his attainments, our open rejection, warmth or withdrawal of love (ignoring him).

I am quite conscious that the methods briefly described here must seem quite unpractical in the case of a *large* nursery school. There contact between the person in charge and the individual child cannot be as close as I have said is desirable, unless she has exceptional ability in this field. But though I do not conceal the difficulties in a large nursery school and am conscious that my point of view is based on theoretical studies and their testing in a *small* nursery school, I still consider it the right general aim in the children's interest. Ideas must not be suppressed because unfavourable circumstances oppose them. It is for us, as far as possible, to mould external circumstances according to our wishes, and where this is impossible, the ideal should still be kept in mind as one possible to realise in the future.

It will have appeared from the previous argument that the large nursery school is unfavourable to small children. The educator of old who was not psychologically minded, was mostly conscious, even though for other reasons, of the disadvantages of a large community for a small child. Various attempts were made to counteract the damaging effects of a large group, and instead of large classes small groups, uniting a few children in a family of sorts, were organised.* If it were possible to have one person in charge of each group (group-mother) the ideal state would be reached, as under these circumstances the transference situation would be suitably initiated.† Unfortunately group nursery schools can only be begun where the help of students is available. By a constant change of students, the children are continually brought into contact with new people, and being exposed to the most varied guidance. Firm emotional relationships are made more difficult, and a good transference of the children to the teacher is made very difficult. It seems questionable to me whether a larger nursery school under the influence of *one* leader without the help of many students, has not fewer disadvantages for children than a group nursery school exposed to unrest and aimlessness. It is not the object of this book to find a solution for this problem, just as I am unable to say more about the training of nursery school teachers within the framework of this book, although much might be said on this point from the psychoanalytical point of

* First by Henriette Schrader-Breymann in the Pestalozzi-Froebel House, Berlin, 1898.

† The group system was carried out in the best possible way by Anna Freud in "the residential war nurseries" she founded in London during the Second World War. Here among other things, an opportunity was also given to make psychological observations on the children's reactions. The relationships of the children with their "foster mothers" illustrate the course of the transference or in the case of motherless children the development of emotions for the first time. The short book *Infants without Families: the Case for and against Residential Nurseries*, by Dorothy Burlingham and Anna Freud, arising out of this work, is extraordinarily stimulating.

view. The only purpose of these remarks is to draw attention to the question.

Now the transference situation, so important from the educational point of view, must be examined more closely. So far as the child's later attitude to persons in authority over him, especially his schoolmasters, is concerned, it is surely of the greatest importance how the transference develops in the nursery school. If the child adopts an attitude of opposition, his resistance may easily be transferred to his school; on the other hand it may be assumed that time successfully spent in the nursery school may be a good preparation for school. Such lasting effects of the nursery school may of course only be taken into consideration if a *long* period at the *same* nursery school may be counted on. It is generally overlooked how dangerous for a child a frequent change of teachers can be, and how damaging it is to remove a child from an environment where he was beginning to take root. The shocks to which a child's "love life" is exposed, may influence the development of his whole personality. Fear of loss of love and of disappointments may come to be the basis of his whole personality.*

One might well ask now whether difficulties which might be considered due to a transference-attachment may not appear when the child is leaving the nursery school. I have found that such lasting attachments to the nursery school happen in only a very few cases.

---

* It may be pointed out here that the change of a nurse, frequent changes of domestic helps or the loss of a loved nanny may have the same effect. Perhaps the unavoidable change of persons in an institution (holidays and working days divided into shifts) may be one of the causes, according to recent observations, why children develop less favourably in the best institutions than those cared for by a family. The small child's need for a relationship to a "near you" is initiated with far less hindrance if he is looked after on his own in a foster family.

The Running of the Nursery School

Even where the child seems greatly attached to the nursery school, or where there were close ties to the person in charge or to one of the children, distress at parting is overcome surprisingly quickly. Entrance into a school means a longed-for step towards growing-up, and the nursery school is felt to have been a stage that has been left behind. The child's repudiation of the nursery school and his previous playmates on entering school may be put down partly to this. But it should not be overlooked that the gesture of superiority may also be understood as an overcompensation for the pain at separation.

If a strong nostalgia for the nursery school period is noticeable in a child, I tend to view this as a neurotic symptom, unless it arises out of difficulties at school. A normal child has the urge to go forward; where there is a tendency to look back, it should be observed as a tendency to regression (25).

It may of course happen that by the attitude of the person in charge, the child will be driven into a violent attachment, greater than is either desirable or necessary to obtain a transference. Presumably many nursery school teachers or nannies, who overwhelm one child or a group of children with an excess of love, are not aware of the implications of their behaviour, or even of the existence of their excessive love. Psychoanalytical discoveries have led to a new view of the question of choice of profession, and the attitude of a person to, and in, his work has also come to be understood in terms of his unconscious. The behaviour of the teacher is influenced as much by his own childhood experiences, the traces of which are deeply embedded in his emotional life, as by the experiences and thoughts of the present day. Emotions and feelings that could not be canalised in

87

Psychology in the Nursery School

real life have effects on our behaviour with children. Sexual tendencies and unfulfilled maternal feelings, among others, find expression here and find substitutive satisfaction and desirable sublimation in work with children. It needs self-observation, however, and above all knowledge of these matters to preserve us from deviations.*

That unconscious factors also contribute to many of the teacher's difficulties cannot be emphasised strongly enough. Quite a number of teachers suffer from occasional disciplinary difficulties. The failure of a child, or the resistance of a group of children, frequently insults the narcissism (26) of a teacher, even though he may be consciously detached. The children's reactions are taken to be the results of his own mistakes, are regarded as revelations of his faults and therefore constituting an insult to him. Ambitious grown-ups take it badly when they see that children do not take the path prescribed for them. Here one can see how much greater are the difficulties of the modern teacher: a teacher of the old school *wished* to rule, and the modern teacher rejects this desire, but his unconscious plays unpleasant tricks on him by letting its manifestions speak too openly. When Therese Simon mentions the dual existence of the child, we might enlarge on this and speak of the teacher's dual existence.

The modern teacher too sometimes gives way to an unconscious urge to plague a child, although he might consciously reject such action. The wish for power,

* On this point see Nelly Wolffheim, *Psychologische Anmerkungen ueber den Erzieherberuf*". Psyche, Jahrbuch fuer Tiefenpsychologie und Menschenkunde in Forschung und Praxis. 1 Jahrg. 3 lieferung 1948, Verlag Lambert Schneider, Heidelberg—and *The Profession of the Educator*, The New Era in Home and School, Vol. 30, No. 5, May 1949.

sadism (27), and much else may be added factors. Perhaps it was just these urges that made the teacher choose his profession, though unconsciously of course, and hidden outwardly by convincing and attractive reasons. It might be remembered that excessive kindness can be a compensation for cruelty and that softness even in education may cover sadistic impulses.

The role of mainly unconscious guilt-feelings among teachers should be emphasised. Wherever the teacher feels his own weak spot, or just senses it, he will be intolerant towards the child. He does not want the same faults to develop, especially not in a child whom he loves.

In most cases it is the love of children that brings grown-ups to occupy themselves with them. What, however, lies in the unconscious behind this conscious love? Surely, the love of children comes from identification with them. Only those, who even though unconsciously, can put themselves in the child's place will have any real affection for him. Longings from one's own childhood, and frequently one's own suffering, form the basis of the desire to help; as an educator one wants to improve children's conditions so that they are better off than one has been oneself. In the choice of the teaching and educational profession, opposition to one's own parents or teachers will often play a part, though only in very few cases does this idea emerge from the unconscious. The wish to reform arises mostly from unconscious drives, rooted in the relationship with one or other parent. Doubtless these motives, where they are the background to the choice of a profession, may lead the teacher to a kind of interference, which he may not favour consciously, and from this conflicts may arise; where a socio-political point of view, the desire to spread ideas, to establish a new point of view, is the basic motive for educational interests, conflicts may arise even more. Here the danger that the child may be treated as a mere cipher is obvious, and the wish to be his leader may come to the surface, though consciously an authoritarian system of education is rejected.

Out of the struggle between conscious aims and the unconscious streams of the emotional life difficulties may arise from which the teacher suffers without recognising their cause. Most states of physical or emotional exhaustion that may be observed frequently among nursery school teachers, are caused not only by the actual overwork, but by these inner difficulties.* Increasing bitterness, irritability towards children and unconscious dislike of working with them can often be observed. These symptoms should not be ignored, both in the interest of the children who may have to suffer from being superintended so unsuitably, and in the interest of the teacher herself. In many cases I should recommend counteracting this exhausting struggle by psychoanalysis. Let it be emphasised that apart from the subjective condition of the teacher, the educational work also benefits from analysis. We can confront the child quite differently if our outlook has been enlarged by psychoanalytical knowledge. It is even desirable (if not at present practical) to include psychoanalysis in the training for the teaching profession. If current attempts to shorten the duration of analysis are successful, there is the prospect that more analyses can be carried out than before. For teacher and child this would open up new possibilities. The experiments in "group analysis" carried out in recent years are another attempt

* This point is made from observations in Germany.

to give analytical insight to a wider circle and to lessen individual difficulties. The "depth psychology course for social workers and teachers" held in Berlin since 1947 is from our point of view a desirable enlargement of professional training.

CHAPTER VII

PLAY AND OCCUPATIONS
IN THE NURSERY SCHOOL

The teacher who is psychoanalytically minded considers play and occupations *freely carried out* the focal point of nursery school life. It was the achievement of Maria Montessori to introduce self-occupation for children into the nursery school. It was the intention in Froebel's Kindergarten also to instruct children how to occupy themselves, but by means of giving advice (not only technical), by stimulating their ideas, by precise directions how they should be carried out; briefly, letting the children work under the guidance of the teacher instead of their own, it was shown that the true meaning of self-occupation had not yet been understood. The revolutionary change in occupational methods made by Montessori has had an influence also on nursery schools run on Froebel's lines. Here also the children are nowadays allowed freedom in work and play, and the method used earlier of occupying the children within a time-table has gradually been abandoned. To-day nursery schools can be found where children are allowed even greater freedom of choice than in those run on Montessori lines, for the latter undo some of the good they do by prescribing how the materials are to be used and by ignoring imaginative play. We completely agree with Susan Isaac when she writes: "Finally it is a wise general rule to leave the children free to use their playthings in their own way—even if that does not happen to be the way that we might think the best. For play has the greatest value for the young child when it is really free and his own."*

Why psychoanalytical education tries to guide the child towards independence we have seen already—independent occupation of the child is a pre-requisite of his independence. It also seems probable to me that a real sublimation, for which the nursery school should afford the child occasion, will succeed more easily through occupations devised by the child himself than through prescribed tasks where the child cannot follow his own impulses. The child gives expression to whatever he is emotionally preoccupied with—whether he does this by actual playing or by an occupation like drawing, painting, modelling, or cutting out from paper. If we leave him liberty to illustrate his instinctual urges, his emotions, his thoughts, we help him to a better "coping with the impressions life makes on him" (*Bewältigung seiner Lebenseindruecke*—Freud).

If one observes a child left to his own devices, most often one will see him playing. The normal child looks for and finds a way to occupy himself in playing. Even if no real toys are available, and no other material that might be used as such, the child will not give up playing. He will play in his thoughts, imagining adventures for himself, and daydream. For this also is play. Play means a transformation of reality, a wish-fulfilment, an occupation with oneself. The value of play for the child is based on several instinctual forces. Above all the child tries to gain pure pleasure from play. He often portrays something that seems remote from his daily life and unknowingly gives himself a part which fulfils consciously, and even more unconsciously, his desires.

* S. Isaacs. *The Nursery Years*, p. 133.

Instincts repressed by education, displaced wishes, and secret impulses come into the open during play. For a child may do unpunished in play what in real life he is forbidden to do; what is forbidden may be experienced here in permitted form without coming into conflict with the child's super-ego, and unnoticed by those around.

"The family game" considered in this light is one where the child identifies himself with his father or mother and is thus able to satisfy the Œdipus-wishes active within his imagination. The "children" appearing in this game represent in many cases brothers or sisters who can here be dominated, punished and tortured as much as one likes. The will to power and the desire to be someone of importance may be expressed in play. It can be imagined that children who are suppressed in real life and have to suffer from fear, or feelings of inferiority and inhibitions, give themselves over to power fantasies in play and feel great and superior in it. In this context various fighting and war-games come to mind; in these the child may threaten, tie up and beat up others, or he can be the powerful one and dominate the others. With timid children, especially, I have often observed the overcompensation of their fears in this kind of game. Being opposed to war, we shall of course never invite children to play war games, but we should beware of suppressing their love of fighting when this tends to emerge in their play. The instinct to fight is effective in all of us. The discharge of affects which is achieved in these games is an aid to the child and too strong a repression of them which is often the result of educational influences may in some children cause an accumulation of affects—something that is bad in any case. Probitions inhibiting play should therefore be avoided. Acts of cruelty against a doll or a woolly toy are best ignored; it seems probable that affects which find an outlet in play, may prevent trouble in real life. We deceive ourselves if we believe that any attempt to influence a playing child with moral advice will really be able to change him.

Our own views should not lead us to cut down the child's freedom of play. If for example in some circles fairy tale games are suppressed because they are not in accord with the parent's outlook, this must be rejected from our point of view. There are children who are especially fond of this type of game and who want to be prince or princess again and again to nourish their desire for power and their narcissism. We saw that the child needs the imaginative transformation of his wishes in order to be able to adjust himself to reality. To exclude fairy tale figures, whether in stories or acted plays, means robbing the children of the oldest known symbols for their profoundest conflicts. Finally nothing will be achieved by this rejection, as children create figures in their own imaginations and it is immaterial what names they give them.

Nor should playing with bricks be forgotten here, as it gives occasion for the expression of emotional experiences and lines of thought. There are children who for some lengthy period will repeatedly represent fire, the collapse of a house, collisions—in short, destruction. At the same time their drawings and spoken fantasies express the same and make it clear that their emotions are repressed. It also seems evident that the building of lavatories popular with many children and usually explained with a delighted grin reveals anal interests discussed elsewhere. THEO for example showed me how secret aggressive instincts can break through in play. He

95

was jealous, it seemed to me rightly so, of his little sister, and knew how to hide his emotions. But while he was playing with toy bricks, he revealed his true feelings and his wishes, which were directed against her. He explained to me what he had built in the following manner: "That's a bed and a doll is lying in it. She was naughty and went to the window. There now I put stones on her and now she is dead. Now comes the hearse." The small boy was grinning all over his face as he spoke the last words. As on the previous day an exciting scene had occurred in THEO'S nursery when the mother saw that both children had climbed up on the window-sill, one must assume that the boy carried on his game from this position and that the child in bed was meant to be his sister, against whom his apparently unconscious death-wishes were directed. Thus the deepest emotional secrets are frequently revealed during the child's games.

The very common game of being a doctor should not remain unmentioned in this connection. The unconscious reasons for it may differ, but it can often be assumed that the medical treatments in the play are a symbolic representation of sexual processes. It might further be remembered how tirelessly dolls are taken to the lavatory and have their nappies changed. This is played also by boys with great zest, and presumably the child's early memories in being educated for cleanliness or the unconscious after-effects of this process—especially in cases of only children—may well be the basis of this game. This may be taken as proof of how deeply education in personal cleanliness affects a child's mind and it can be seen that fixations which outwardly seem to have been overcome, may still exist.

It may easily be observed that children form their own feelings of tenderness when they play with dolls (or with teddy bears and similar cloth animals). A closer investigation than has so far appeared in publications of child analyses ought to be made on what dolls mean in the child's unconscious and what importance they have as symbols. The doll as an object of love can give the child in his emotional life the chance to care for it, to be tender to it; and as the child most probably believes that he is also loved by the doll, his need for love will be satisfied. It is valuable for the person in charge of the nursery school to observe how the child plays with his dolls, whether the child longs for more love, whether he would like to be more tender than he is allowed to be, or is capable of being according to his personality.

These few examples have shown how much is recognisable from the child's play. The observer, however, understands a part only of what is expressed in play—in a sense only the upper layer—as the greater part is not expressed directly but in symbolic form; the important and essential parts can only be deciphered with the help of analytical understanding. The one issue we have tried to clear up with our few remarks is this: what is important in the child's emotional life, what, predominantly unconsciously, worries him, what may be the cause of inner struggles or pleasure—all these are expressed in the child's play.*

* In this connection some sentences of Melanie Klein's might be quoted. They show on the one hand how play is observed and used in child analysis and how in her opinion, in agreement with our view, it may lead to a better understanding of the child also outside analysis:

"The analyst gets his material in a very specific way. The attitude he shows to the child's associations and games is entirely free from ethical and moral criticism. This is indeed one of the ways in which a transference can be established and analysis set going. Thus the child will show to the analyst what it would never reveal to his mother or nurse, for good reasons. They would be very much shocked to notice aggression or asocial tendencies against which education is mostly directed. Moreover, it is just this analytical work which resolves repression and in this way brings about the manifestations of the un-

97

Psychology in the Nursery School

In order that the child may cope with the conflicts created by life and in particular by his upbringing, the use of his imagination is needed to give him what would otherwise be out of reach. Thus children's play may be called the imaginative experience of their wishes which helps their adjustment to reality. "The creation of the mental domain of fantasy has a complete counterpart in the establishment of 'reservations' and 'nature parks' in places where the inroads of agriculture, traffic, or industry threaten to change the original face of the earth rapidly into something unrecognisable. The 'reservation' is to maintain the old condition of things which has been regretfully sacrificed to necessity everywhere else; there everything may grow and spread as it pleases, including what is useless or even harmful. The mental realm of fantasy is also such a reservation reclaimed from the encroaches of the reality principle."* If we regard play from this point of view we shall end by letting the child play a lot. If the small child's freedom to play is restricted it means making his life more difficult. We cannot expect a child to adjust himself to our way of life and keep in step with us culturally without·giving him the opportunity to transform his wishes in fantasies.

It follows from the views here expressed that play as a factor in a child's development must be taken seriously.

conscious. This is obtained slowly, step by step, and some of the games I mentioned have occurred in the course of the analysis, and not at the beginning. It must be added, however, that the children's games even outside the analysis are very instructive and give evidence of many of those impulses which are discussed here. But it requires a specially trained observer, a knowledge of symbolism and psychoanalytic methods in order to ascertain these." "Criminal Tendencies in Normal Children." *The British Journal of Medical Psychology.* VII. Pt. II. 1927. p. 182.

* S. Freud. *Introductory Lectures on Psychoanalysis.* Allen & Unwin, London. pp. 311–312.

Play and Occupations

The usual subordination of play to "work" at school and the "occupations" of the small child (in the sense of Froebel and Montessori) must be considered harmful to the child. Whether it is more valuable for the young child to occupy himself with educational or constructional materials or to express himself by playing freely, is a question we answer in favour of play. The nursery school teacher should try to enlighten parents, to inform them of the value of play and to counter the objection so frequently heard: "Why should I send my child to the nursery school where he plays all the time and learns nothing?" I am inclined to believe the child should be given opportunities for both forms of occupation, and be allowed to choose without any external pressure according to his mood at a given moment.

The neglect of active imagination in Montessori's system will therefore appear a serious mistake. It is impossible here to state in detail our view in opposition to that of Montessori. It should, however, be pointed out how fundamentally our ideas of imaginative play, based on a psychoanalytical viewpoint, differ from hers. With us it is not a question whether and how to DEVELOP the child's imagination by special measures (organised play or occupations) as in the older type of Froebel Kindergarten. Our interest is directed to the *possibility of undisturbed play at all times* in the nursery school, as well as the children's freedom to give way to their fantasies and to experience them in their play. Of course we shall try to give the child alternative values if he tends excessively towards day-dreaming and too fantastic games; but we do not believe that such a re-direction towards reality, as far as that is possible by educational games and materials, is the only way of treating such an abnormal condition. In cases like that we

99

take into account that a symptom is coming into operation, and its particular cause should be investigated.
"Play is the highest phase of child development—of
human development at this period; for it is self-active
representation of the inner representation of the inner
necessity and impulse."*

The discoveries of psychoanalysis made us regard an
inhibition in playing to be a preliminary step to an inhibition of the capacity to work (M. Klein). This con-
firms the view expressed by Froebel: "A child that plays
thoroughly, with self-active determination, persever-
ingly until physical fatigue forbids, will surely be a
thorough, determined man, capable of self-sacrifice
for the promotion of himself and others."†

Thus it seems an important task of the nursery school
to give children who do not want to play—who are, in
other words, unable to play—the capacity to do so. But
of course how to influence a child in this direction cannot
be easily laid down. There are many diverse kinds of
neurotic inhibitions that prevent a child from playing.
Excessive repressions, unconscious guilt feelings, and
above all a tendency to self-punishment, seem to be
capable of impeding play. Some aggressions expressed
in play may frighten the "well-brought-up" child, for
they become conscious during his play and he will then
not permit himself to express himself freely by his play.
Children tending to depression sometimes take refuge in
play to free themselves from their disquieting thoughts;
but frequently these very depressions will be the cause
of playing badly, as they prevent the child from relaxing
in play and do not allow him to let his imagination run
freely. In some of these cases psycho-analytic treat-

* and † F. Froebel. *The Education* of *Man.* D. Appleton & Co.,
New York and London, 1912, p. 54–55.

ment can be of real help. I have already shown how important this may be for the development of the personality, especially when the connection between inhibition of play and work is remembered.

But one may not always want to have recourse to treatment, and the question is what remedies there are at hand to help the child. In my experience contact with other children has good results, especially where, as in the nursery school, removal from the domestic environment takes place. But even if the child is introduced to other children, one should always behave passively, and his friends should never be prescribed to him. Any interference which may seem to the child intentional will easily evoke resistance and opposition. If the teacher remains passive, and the child is drawn into play by other children and the whole atmosphere is pleasant and distracting, success may frequently be observed. Impatience will not do, and active interference should only come after waiting for a long time. In those cases the teacher had best play with the child carefully but without any hint of condescension, then gradually withdraw and leave the child alone in his game. Above all, children who are inhibited about playing must be shown that in their play nothing is rejected or thought unusual. If the child recognises our encouragement he will be less afraid to reveal what is hidden. A conversation touching the child's emotional life, loosening his unconscious and removing repressions may make the child readier to play—this remedy will, however, be at the disposal only of a psychoanalytically trained teacher.

It is known that occupations carried out from a specific point of view may have therapeutic value. From the psychoanalytical point of view the occasional successes will be taken as the resolution of symptoms, which is very useful in some cases without, of course, ending the deeper-lying neurosis. I myself have succeeded several times through occupational therapy applied to individual children giving them more self-assurance, in ending certain active inhibitions, in stimulating the desire to work, in inducing calmness, etc.; but these partial successes should never result in our neglecting the continuance of perhaps less obvious symptoms.

In connection with play it must be mentioned again that according to my experience the small child is often not capable of playing with other children until the end of its fourth year, even though it may like being with them. So playing alone is not something abnormal leading one to believe that the child is a potential hermit or asocial, but seems to me the result of the child's need to create his own fantasies exclusively. It may also be a result of the child's urge to develop, so that at this stage the child wants only to experience himself unhampered by outside influences. As a result of this assumption grown-ups will only play with the child on exceptional occasions. The adult who plays too often with a child robs him of opportunities of development and he inhibits his imagination and initiative. Some children lose the ability to play out of inner experience, if grown-ups participate too much in their play. (This has often been observed with children who have a nurse to themselves.) Besides there are few adults only who know how to put themselves into the background while playing with the child, and who can leave all initiative to him. We must remember that those adults who know best how to play with children identify themselves strongly with them. In this process the educative importance of play which we have stressed is easily forgotten. Then the adult unconsciously carries his own wishes and fantasies into the play and thus stifles the child's activities. I was told of a young girl whose analysis later revealed that she had brought an entire wish-complex to bear on her mother-and-child game with children. This was so vivid and far removed from reality that she awoke as if she had been dreaming when the play was interrupted.

So far only games thought out by children themselves and arising out of their fantasies have been mentioned. Now it is proposed to examine dancing and singing games, which are not really free games but are carried out according to certain rules accompanied by words and music. Quite apart from the child's pleasure in rhythm and movement, there is something in these games that moves the child's unconscious strongly. It can be seen from the popularity of a game whether it is suitable for a group of children. I consider it quite mistaken to force the child to participate in a game of movement, still customary in a number of nursery schools, because it is considered useful for his social education (community games equal community spirit). The child's emotional life is only touched if he likes to play. Play carried on against the child's will is absurd, an additional pressure in the child's life, producing the opposite result to what is intended: an inner reluctance and despite external adjustment another unpleasant experience of the compulsions of education. Social adjustment will only be initiated by living in a community of children, not by the artificial organisation of games.

Some games are popular with nearly all children. Where rhyme and rhythm are not the moving element, it must presumably be the content of the game which strongly affects the child's emotions and in some manner gives expression to his wishes or difficulties.* In the choice of community games we should therefore follow the children's proposals and be guided by them. If there is resistance when practising a new game—and children in a freely-led nursery school will show this easily—it should not be ignored. Æsthetic considerations should not come too much to the foreground here. From the educational point of view there is undoubtedly a danger in community games that the person in charge may put herself and her intentions too much in the limelight, so that the initiative does not come from the children. Whether she is guided by external reasons (e.g., the effect of games on spectators, practising with an eye to end-of-term displays in the nursery school) or whether games are thought valuable for creating communal ties or to keep a large group occupied, in few nurseries is there playing as we should like it to be. The bored expressions of the participants are a comment on this abuse of what is called "play".

But rhythmic games may be a beautiful experience for children and beneficial for their minds and bodies. It just depends whether the games are conducted in the right way. Primarily it depends on the ability of the teacher, to create gaiety and rhythm, and above all to secure the children's willing participation. Real attention will be best achieved where the children are not just imitating and carrying out a game according to rules, but where they are encouraged to create for themselves. The ideal would be an arrangement by which creation, execution, even music and rhythm were left to the children's inventiveness, thus creating the game in their

* Here the interesting work of Sigmund Pfeifer (Budapest) on "Auesserung Infantil-erotischer Triebe im Spiel" should be pointed out. Imago V. 1917–1919. p. 243.

company. Such a kind of play can of course be considered only for a small group led by someone with great ability, but it would be in accord with what we consider desirable for the children also in other respects.

We do not want to prevent the children playing an occasional community game according to the mood of the moment, but in it we want to let them participate in an active not a passive role. It was previously mentioned that to force a child to participate should not be allowed, and it should now be added that in some cases such pressure may be harmful. If some children refuse to play in community games, their refusals to join the circle may sometimes point to fears coming from the unconscious which may not be understood without further examination. In connection with this it would be desirable if more material from child-analyses was available, to bring enlightenment and help us to understand children's behaviour. In a case that became known to me a circle of children moving along and holding on to each other, seemed to a single child, who was refusing to join them, a mass that would swallow him. In another case symbolic interpretation was not necessary, the child was simply afraid that he might be dragged to the ground. In one nursery school it became clear one day how strong these fears can be, when a child, who had been clearly reluctant to join a circle, was forced to do so and then fell down in the middle of it and rolled on the floor in fits, crying. The school teacher had tried to break his "stubbornness"!

Now that we have tried to illuminate play and its importance, it will be our task to deal with the other occupations usual in the nursery school.

Apart from guiding the child towards the community his general education is also considered our duty. As

Psychology in the Nursery School

Froebel says: "The purpose of the Kindergarten is not only to supervise children, but to give them occupations according to their personalities, to exercise their senses and to occupy their awakening minds; to acquaint them intimately with nature and the world of man, especially to guide heart and emotions in the right way, to the basic purpose of life, i.e., communion with them. In their play they should live joyously and in many directions, using and developing all their powers in blameless serenity, unity and pious childliness. They should really prepare themselves for school and the coming stages of life like plants growing in a garden with God's blessing and the gardener's careful supervision."*

Montessori agrees with these views and writes: "This is not simply a place where the children are kept, not just an asylum, but a true school for their education, and its methods are inspired by the rational principles of scientific pedagogy. The physical development of the children is followed, each child being studied from the anthropological standpoint. Linguistic exercises, a systematic sense training, and exercises which directly fit the child for the duties of practical life, form the basis of the work done."†

It goes without saying that the psychoanalytically-minded nursery school teacher will also bear the child's preparation for school and life in mind, even though we consider the latter of greater importance and emphasise this clearly by placing adjustment to reality in the forefront of our nursery school education.

Above all, those occupations will be offered which give children an opportunity for free activity and self-expression, and in that way form the basis for sublima-

* Froebels Schriften, Vol III, Berlin 1862–3. p. 469.
† *The Montessori Method*, p. 62–3. Heinemann, London, 1920.

tion. For my purposes I found most useful of all free-drawing, painting and modelling, cutting out from paper, and other paperwork in conjunction with painting and building. Apart from that I found various colour games, and the stringing of pearls, to be calming occupations, making for concentration and popular with the children. Large movable bricks of wood are especially important. With all this the vital thing is to let each child find what corresponds to his development and mood at that moment. It is immaterial if the advancement of the child's intellect, senses or skill, desirable as this is, is thereby put into the background. A difficulty in allowing free choice of occupations is of course that by imitation children approximate too much to each other, which often brings a false choice with it. Here the skill of the person in charge comes in to guide the child to a genuine decision. A task of greater importance than all others is the development of the child's personality and the increase of its initiative and will-power. For this the creation of possibilities to sublimate seems to me the most important thing in this age group.

If during a period of powerful instinctual renunciation, or while suffering from an accumulation of affects due to the Œdipus situation, a child transfers his emotional drives with the help of a suitable occupation, we can contribute something of greater value during this period than by giving the child occasion to form a colour sense or to develop his intellectual powers. For example HANS (aged 5)—who illustrated destructive events in his drawings: the burning of a ship, the collapse of a house and similar events—not only gives us glimpses of his emotional processes but himself finds a way with the aid of these creative efforts to bring an inner experience into the open. Analogous to the creation of the artist something is produced out of the realm of thought and emotion and is in a way converted into something of greater value. Such an unconscious connection with a predominant interest seemed to be the case with HEIN-RICH's modelling. Aged 5, he modelled a pudding and put a long "custard tube" into the middle which he bent forward. He explained to me "custard is going to come out of there on to everyone's plate". He replied to my somewhat astonished question whether he had ever seen such a tube before, by pointing rather shyly to his trousers, "well, in front". This symbolic reproduction contained for the child the experience of emotionally important facts. The drawing of ALEX (aged 6) repro-duced most clearly what was occupying his interest at that time. In his development the boy was still in the anal stage and his thoughts were concentrated on dirt and excrement in a manner unusual for his age. He always drew animals and human beings with excrement falling from them, and drew people, characteristically only those he was particularly fond of, up to their waist, wading in black dirt. When a friend of his had drawn a man, ALEX committed a glaring transgression; he added everything to the drawing that seemed to him to have been forgotten—a urinating penis, dirt coming out of nose and ear. For this boy this form of pictorial abreac-tion was a visible relief. At his home such doings would have been taken very much amiss; he always came to the nursery school exceptionally clean and well turned out, and because of his good upbringing would have been ashamed to use an unclean word. When he noticed that I was not horrified by his drawings (as happened at his home), he always looked at me with an air of gleeful conspiracy and seemed pleased that I left him in peace. I was sure that just this reproduction of his secretive interest would lead to it being less outstanding in his emotional life and gradually to its dying down altogether.

To make use of children's drawings with the help of psychoanalytical interpretation is a task to which the psychoanalytically-trained teacher could well make contributions. Scientific use of the material would increase our knowledge of child psychology considerably. As far as I know no work from a Freudian psychologist exists on this subject. Among the followers of Jung there is, however, a great interest in the paintings of children, which are of course interpreted quite differently from us. An illustrated book by Michael Fordham, *The Life of Childhood, a Contribution to Analytical Psychology* (Kegan Paul, Trench Trubner & Co., London, 1944) should be mentioned here.

The sublimation of anal instincts seems to me to be of great importance for children of the nursery school age. Elsewhere the strength of the tension between educational influence and unconscious forces has been mentioned. The child can be helped over this if given the opportunity for an occupation that can create an equilibrium. Modelling will be specially useful for that. If the children are allowed to use the modelling material without direction in the beginning they will do nothing but play with it aimlessly, press the whole mass, rub it into sausages and perhaps tear it to pieces. Gradually out of this unconscious blind activity, a more conscious creativeness emerges, figures are produced from imagination or copied from objects that arouse interest. GERT (aged 4) although mentally he had not yet reached that age, proved to me how strongly clay resembles excrement to smaller children. He called his modelling material "horrids", pulled small pieces from it, smelt them and put them into a corner of the room. He held such a piece under my nose and said, "and now I'm going to make the bottom where it came out".

Stick-on paper games help the same tendency. In the beginning the child is quite indifferent to the result of sticking the paper on with a particular purpose and to the creation of patterns. The "educative" hint that neatness is essential is often quite ignored. Sometimes smudges are even thought desirable and are often made artificially and rubbed all over the paper. Gradually here too work with a definite purpose will develop. Playing with sand and splashing water about also give the primitive love of dirt an opportunity to be sublimated. From grubbing about in the sand, mixing sand and water and covering themselves with this mixture (where up-bringing does not interfere) children will gradually progress to conscious activity, making mountains, caves and tunnels. Sand and water games, particularly sand cakes baked often with great intensity and the frequent splashing of water, seem to have a special symbolic meaning. Without the symbolism lying behind them, these primitive occupations, which appear so monotonous to an observer, would hardly have such powers of attraction for children all over the world.

Painting with colours may also counter the child's anal wishes. Even three-year-olds in the nursery school like to paint with colours and spread them about. Here the "messing about" gives pleasure and is in the beginning done quite without any sense of colour or composition. The gradual creativeness can surely be seen as a sublimation of the initial love to smudge and make a mess. Despite conscious creativeness pleasure in putting on masses of colour can be observed continuing for a long time. Perhaps it is in recognition of this pleasure that in some nursery schools in England paints are not put on with brushes but with the fingers.*

It might be of interest to mention that the predominance of anal interest which the middle-class children of my nursery school showed does not seem to be so strongly noticeable in working-class children. I draw this conclusion from an informative collection of drawings shown to me by the psychoanalytically-minded director of a working-class nursery school. There the illustration of sexual relations and interest in genitals and sexuality in general was emphasised. It might be assumed that the preoccupation with anal matters, and a more lasting interest in them, is connected with that early and strict suppression which in middle-class circles is expected from even very small children. On the other hand a child from these circles has fewer opportunities to make his own observations on sexual matters. This does not mean, however, that middle-class children are not pre-occupied with sexual matters and do not also express them—but according to my experience they do not do it so predominantly.

If we regard the occupation of children in the way outlined here, all guiding, stimulating and prescribing of activities must seem wrong. Occasional tasks, or better even suggestions, are justified, but the rule should be *independent choice and execution of occupations by the children themselves*, and we should interfere only if the child needs this help. Usually, however slowly, he will find his own way or will profit by the example of other children. Some children are very fond of being given stimulating ideas and encouragement. If we intend to

* Frederick H. Allen in *Psychotherapy with Children* (Kegan Paul, Trench, Trubner, London) mentions a book by Ruth Shaw *Finger Painting* (Little, Brown, Boston) which deals with children's paintings of this sort.

help in this way, the play we suggest must be such as can be executed by the children. With some children insecurity, laziness and a wish for signs of affection lie behind repeated requests for suggestions or help. Here we must pay careful attention to what may be the cause, so as to be able to offer the child help instead of simply complying with his wish, which may sometimes be more hindrance than help. All formal set occupations seem unsuitable (apart from the daily tasks that are part of the domestic life of the nursery school). That unrestricted occupational methods also give children opportunities to develop, to practise their skills, and to increase their mental ability—and that this seems important to me even if not predominantly—should be mentioned as a precaution here. It should also be emphasised that emotional qualities are by no means disregarded by us, although we only occasionally work in groups or for one another, and although we let these qualities develop spontaneously out of the atmosphere in our school and not out of organised occupations. Nor am I ignoring the importance of occasional communal handicraftwork done by a group of children, since I have learnt to value it as a stimulus and a source of joy; if it is not done at the children's own suggestion, it should be suggested only occasionally.

Respect for the child's individual existence does not seem to me sufficiently emphasised. Thus Froebel's dictum "the child should learn to make subjective experience objective" is interpreted wrongly in many nursery schools. An objective experience, even if it interests the child and makes him happy, is not necessarily of the importance to the child which his teachers think it is, and will not always become a subjective experience. Thus it seems to me that earlier systems of running nursery schools were mistaken in thinking they saw in the representation of impressions an "objectivisation of the child's emotional life". The emotional life of a child only expresses itself by representation, or by living through what has been experienced (*Darlebung*) to use Froebel's expression, in free play or in unrestricted occupation free from external suggestions.*

Since Freud's depth-psychology has taught us to look at the child in a new way it is known that the interests, wishes and moods of individual children differ widely. Behind the external behaviour of the child which we can recognise, his unconscious is effective and influencing him. Only in the rarest cases will it be possible to create any real unity and real co-operation among the children. Either children take part mechanically in a planned task given to them, without being emotionally involved in it, or they take part eagerly but ignore their own inclinations, which, as regards the development of their individual personalities, is not always desirable. Certainly young children should not be put under mental guidance; everything should rather develop by itself and from inside, otherwise there may be faulty or a "hothouse" development. Our task can only consist of making the means of education available to the child.

It seems to me mistaken that things meant for his occupation should be given to him for any specific purpose, thought out by grown-ups (Froebel, Montessori). We must beware of seeing a seemingly point-

* Melanie Klein who has been able to gain wide experience in her child-analyses in respect of child's play (she founded "play analysis") wrote: "Those who are familiar with the play-life of children know that this play-life is entirely concerned with the child's impulse-life and desires, performing them and fulfilling them through his fantasies. From reality, to which it is apparently more or less well adapted, the child takes only as much as is absolutely essential." *Criminal Tendencies*, p. 187.

less effort in a child's activities just because it is not what we had in mind when we gave him the original material. Further it must not be assumed that the child will always do what is intended with the material. The child who apparently purposefully discharges the task prescribed by or arising out of the material, is frequently following his own inclinations and is somehow using it according to his own wishes. As an example the concentric cylinders devised by Montessori will serve. This occupation was particularly popular with three- to five-year-olds, and was frequently chosen by children in the nursery school. It seemed popular because the problem was comparatively simply solved and also because many different games could be played with them. The pieces to be fitted in became human beings, animals, pieces of baggage, etc., in the child's imagination; one day the box is a ship, another a train. Thus the material will not always be used for the task intended by Montessori but will so to speak be turned into something suitable for each individual child; the educational toy is treated like a plaything. While using this toy, it is only incidentally that the child gains knowledge of the relationship of sizes, etc.; and calm concentration and application will surely also be found in this method of using the material. Other children seem to enjoy only the business of placing the cylinders in the box. These are usually smaller children, for whom the material was intended originally. Why then are the older ones still so strongly attached to it and use it again and again? There are plenty of other toys. We assume, and for those who think psychoanalytically the assumption is obvious, that the pieces fitting into each other have some symbolic meaning, which is unconscious but may be the reason for the toy's attractiveness. All who are familiar with children know how they like to push and pull things in and out of openings. The toy industry capitalises this tendency in children.

Sometimes children who eagerly occupy themselves with these cylinders have chosen them only to simulate activity; although seemingly busy, they are, as one can see on their faces, daydreaming. While the teacher, pleased with the child's power of concentration, watches how often the operation has been repeated (Montessori reports speak of thirty-two repetitions), the child has not really been occupied with learning but has been day-dreaming. In this way the child has an opportunity to perform an action not welcomed by many teachers, in a permitted form. On the part of psycho-analysts it has been pointed out that frequent repetition of an occupation may show a tendency to obsessional neurosis.

In so strongly supporting the free choice of occupations, we had above all the advancement of the growth of personality in mind. It must be understood that each choice represents an act of will; each decision made by the individual means finding a way out of a different struggle. Self-chosen occupations avoid having to do what is unpleasant, and result in actions in which the child's momentary emotional life can participate. If the child has made a mistake, if he has reached for something that does not gratify him, he is free to look for something new. It should not be thought too anxiously in the nursery school that the child must "learn" to concentrate. Concentration usually comes on its own, if the child has made the right choice. If a normal child is satisfied with his choice, he will carry on with his occupation until tired. If a child who is already used to the nursery school, rushes from one occupation to another and shows much nervous restlessness, then other methods of treating him will bear better fruit, than forcing on the child activities he will only carry out reluctantly.

The most urgent duty of the teacher is to learn to be patient; to wait for developments should be law to her. This especially applies to the nursery school, for the small child being defenceless has to put up passively with our interference in his development.

Of course the independent choice of occupations, which we have shown to be desirable, may also be a burden to some children. There are children who are frightened by the necessity of making up their own minds, who are too hesitant to make clear decisions. Children who are emotionally occupied with other things, may consider the order to choose an occupation for themselves as a disturbance, especially before they have quite understood the potentialities of the material. Some fear of the nursery school or dislike of being there may be caused in the child, perhaps only in the sense of discomfort, because he does not like making his own choice. Of course the child is usually not conscious of this connection, but a five-year-old girl once spoke very clearly on this point. ERIKA had been in my nursery school for about six months. Her whole behaviour was rather passive and she was never really happy. Her mother told me that ERIKA did not like coming to the nursery school. When the family moved to another part of the town, the child went to another nursery school. I met her one day and asked her how she liked it there. "Much better than with you," said the child full of conviction; "with you we always had to do what we wanted to do, here auntie tells us what to do." This was one of the cases which we should have helped by careful guidance, and it shows once again that even the strict carrying out of a good method may not be suitable for an individual child. Fear of impeding the development of personality may lead to ignoring what is necessary for a particular child. Some children must first be shown the way to independence. This will be especially necessary where strict upbringing at home has strongly inhibited the child, and where his super-ego would not even allow him to do what he wanted in the nursery school.

Generally speaking we support all actions, all efforts of the child which lead him to independence and self-reliance. The often hasty help and assistance of grown-ups may harm the child to an unpredictable extent. In her writings Montessori gives many an example of this. Thanks to her we have learnt the disadvantages of mistaken activity by the teacher. The psychoanalytically-minded educator can add others to Montessori's arguments, on the basis of the insight gained by child-analyses (and retrospective analyses of adults) and will compel himself to let the child have his own way and not to undermine his abilities. He will not only do this in respect of the maddening, hitherto unperceived, effect of authoritative interference, but also because of the importance which all the child's free actions have for his self-confidence and ability to face life. It is to be presumed that the development of many a neurosis will be avoided by correct guidance in this direction. Earlier on we pointed out the dangers threatening particularly the only child because he may be too carefully looked after and helped too much. In all respects the nursery school should try to advance the children's independence in carrying out the tasks of everyday life. For that reason work connected with the domestic aspects of the nursery school and various tasks in the garden should be brought within the children's range of interests. Children nearly always like to take part in all practical work, and the wish to equal adults may be an important factor in this. In addition there is the joy of being physically active, of testing one's strength and getting rid of surplus energy. To me it seems doubtful whether children as young as those in the nursery school would wish "to work for the community", and whether being of service to others is of any importance to them. Activity gives the child narcissistic pleasure in his ability and satisfies his urge to be grown up. I am repeatedly convinced of this every year, when after the garden has been planted, weeded and kept in order with much enjoyment the whole summer, the height of pleasure is reached only in autumn when in pulling up the roots of old plants, (work which resembles destruction rather than construction) the children try and show their strength.

The generally known or presumed educational value of the child doing domestic work or helping to nurse animals need not be discussed here. Only the wish is expressed that with the help of a psychoanalytical point of view we try to look beneath the surface and collect information on the child's attitude to any particular occupation in relation to the form of sublimation it presents and the symbolic meaning attached to it. This may be valuable so far as the occupation itself is concerned, and perhaps also in the interest of the study of neuroses. We are for example thinking of the exaggerated love of order in some nursery school children which has the effect of making each chair out of place, each box not standing straight, appear disturbing and requiring to be put right at once. In this the compulsive element often becomes apparent. The exaggerated desire for cleanliness, which may be the beginning of compulsive washing (or the disposition to it) needs our attention. In this connection I remember little RESI. This child was very fond of me and always tried to do what I liked—more so than seemed desirable to me. The only time RESI resisted me was when I tried to make her wear an overall for some work where she was bound to get dirty. This she would not do—the stains on the overall disturbed her. Such and similar symptoms have meaning, their observation and examination is essential if we consider the early discovery of neurotic symptoms one of the tasks of the nursery school. It must be understood of course that it is not occasional observation but only the repeated appearance of unusual behaviour that should cause us to interfere. Especially with domestic occupations we must consider and examine whether faulty emotional developments may be made worse by them, or whether by the joy in work neurotic characteristics may perhaps be directed into different channels. It also remains to be discovered whether this in itself is desirable or may have unfavourable effects. For the teacher all these matters are important, because if his attitude is the wrong one, she may have a bad influence on the child. Think for example of an ambitious child who attaches great importance to the teacher's praise and recognition, and remember the consequences that are bound to occur if his exaggerated cleanliness or love of order are specially praised and therefore increased.

We do not know whether nature study may not have a profound influence on the young child's emotional life; in no case where children show interest should this be neglected (or not followed up). If we take as a guiding principle the requirement to afford the child opportunities but leave the use of them to him, many children will take interest in nature if given the chance to look after plants and animals. Then, however, we should wait until the child's questions indicate his need for instruction. Attempts to instruct at the wrong moment, whether in an emotional or intellectual direction, will be treated as disturbances as well as undesired conversations by the child, and will be rejected emotionally. This should not surprise us; we cannot unravel the unconscious emotional processes and really do not know in most cases what is occupying children at that moment.

In this field of activity our attention will be directed to several individual peculiarities of children which are relevant here. The psychoanalytical nursery school teacher will not treat certain behaviour in the same way as other teachers might. Thus, to give an example, the urge of some children to torture animals is not condemned as a "character fault", but taken as a symptom of unconscious impulses which we like to investigate but will never punish. Experience has always shown that moral teaching alone can only in extremely rare cases do anything to combat cruelty to animals or destructive trends (often directed against flowers as well as animals). Where education through fear is used, or where the child's love for his teacher results in the desire to fulfil her demands, the suppression of sadistic impulses may occur. It may be nothing more than a momentary success, unimportant for the child's future development and perhaps damaging because the expression of an affect is prevented. The full effect of a faulty emotional development arising from the unconscious cannot be recognised in individual cases without further psychoanalytical examination. If there is strong evidence of

Play and Occupations

abnormal sadistic behaviour and excessive love of destruction, an analysis of the child may make understanding and help possible. In the case of occasional outbreaks one should wait for developments, first because such disturbances of the emotional equilibrium will often cease by themselves, and secondly because cruelty to animals and destructive tendencies may arise from the small child not knowing the implications of his actions. The child is not aware of what he is doing and does not differentiate between the living and the dead, recognises no difference between growing and developing things that should be spared by him and those which he may destroy or treat as he likes. He may lack the capacity to identify himself with animals especially, which is the basis of all conscious care and consideration. Supposing himself to be all-powerful, the child may also think of himself as master of the animal. He has learnt from experience that both in play and seriously, people let themselves be teased by him, and so, as a matter of course, he will try out this conduct with animals just the same. It will probably greatly assist the attempt to achieve greater sensitivity towards animals and an emotional tie with them, if the child is shown how to look after them, and allowed do constructive work with plants to counteract his destructive activity.

In looking after animals and plants we have an occupation that leads children to observe and question, and —what is of prime importance to us—to think critically. If children are used to speaking freely, questions will be asked, the answers to which will lead to the child's understanding of sexual matters, which we have learnt to recognise as important.

It is emphasised that the relation to animals, or to a particular animal, is in no way accidental, or a peculiar phenomenon and therefore merits our attention. We must not repeat the mistake so often made by orthodox educationalists, of making a moral judgment on the love of animals, stressing the "kindness" of a particular child. This characteristic, like the faulty development mentioned, can only be regarded as the manifestation of deeper emotional processes. It does not seem to me far wrong for Pfister to assume that an excessive love of animals will arise if the child's relation to human beings is inhibited. Children who suffer much from stern or unloving parents, without finding substitutes in other people or in religion, will turn their tender affections towards animals.* Any excessive pity of animals which tends to be based on identification with them should make us attentive. Further psychoanalytical research should make clear whether we can counteract the child's frequent fear of dogs, horses, chickens, etc., by giving him the opportunity for closer observation and employment with them. In this the nursery school could fulfil an important task, as an opportunity exists here to put material at research workers' disposal. On the other hand we must assume that our influence on the child will be of a predominantly prophylactic nature: what we know well does not frighten us any the less, as a rule. The reasons for anxieties embedded in the unconscious can hardly be removed by external influence, and it will only be possible to cure animal phobia (28) by psychoanalytical treatment.† Recognition of the profound connection between fear and general emotional ex-

* Oskar Pfister. *Die Liebe des Kindes und seine Fehlentwicklungen.* Verlag Bircher, Bern, 1922. p. 137.
† A demonstration of the course of an animal phobia and its cure by psychoanalytical treatment is given to us in Freud's "Analysis of the phobia in a five-year-old boy". *Collected Papers,* Hogarth, 1925. Vol. 3, p. 149. Also reference may be made to Freud's *Inhibitions, Symptoms and Anxiety,* Hogarth, London, 1936.

perience will make us extra careful with disciplinary measures, never to torture a fearful child with compulsion, punishment or other rigorous methods, or even laugh at him. Moral exhortations appealing to a sense of honour are also best avoided. By educational measures of this kind we may place too great a burden on the child and may merely add feelings of guilt or inferiority to an existing fear. Loving attention, helpful understanding talks, or in advanced cases analytical treatment, are recommended. Anxiety symptoms have such a paralysing effect that at all events one should try to ease them in good time.

After having taken the opportunity here to mention fear in the child's life, we will turn to examine the problem of the telling of fairy tales. We want to show what attitude should be adopted towards them from the psychoanalytical point of view, although I want to make it clear that a universal attitude has not yet been agreed on in this matter. When children's play was discussed, the importance of the fairy story for the child's emotional development was pointed out, and now this will be followed up further. We must make up our minds whether we think it desirable or not that fairy stories should be told in the nursery school.

Many modern educationalists reject the telling of fairy stories to small children. Maria Montessori and her pupils are outspoken opponents of fairy tales, mainly because they want to guide children to realistic thinking and to a conscious examination of reality. By them the fairy tale is considered contrary to a logical training and the confusion of the tales is thought to be a burden on the imagination. The untruthfulness which adults show towards a child incapable of criticism, when telling him a fairy tale, is not thought permissible. The fear that the gruesome figures of a story might be upsetting is another reason why fairy tales are rejected even by teachers who do not hold such strong views.

In another place we have pointed out that according to our point of view the child must transform reality in order to be able to cope with its demands, and we have to recognise that fairy tales are an aid to this. Let us take a few examples: When Cinderella has to stay at home, the child sees that other people have to suffer as he does. He will not understand much about balls and the pleasure of dancing and will hardly be able to imagine much of it, but he knows about having to stay at home when others go out. The child will enjoy it when the powers that prohibit are punished; even if not consciously, he harbours a desire for revenge against those in charge of him whom he must obey. The child will be able to abreact such emotions when he identifies himself with Cinderella. The trick played on the strict mother in this fairy tale must be a source of joy to the child. In another tale the child identifies himself with the dwarfs who are in opposition to the powerful ones, the giants. Kings are father-symbols, like the father they have power. They can do what one would like to do oneself: to rule, they are allowed to do with impunity what one wants to do—to punish enemies, i.e., people one does not love, to vanquish them, to take their possessions, and to take the princess home! We have already seen that secret wishes exist in many children to have sole ownership of and to be happily alone with the person one loves. Also the need for hero-worship may contribute to making them fond of certain stories. It may also be assumed that the fear-creating figures of fairy stories—for instance the wolf in Red Riding Hood —excite children and interest them as much as they do because the dormant fears in the child are transferred to them. Identification of self with the characters in fairy tales may be a further factor. The child puts himself in the place of the wolf, committing cruelties which attract the child from unconscious sources.

While it is claimed that fairy tales make adjustment to the demands of life more difficult, because they obscure the clear view of it, our examples show just the opposite and allow the fairy tale to be an aid to the adjustment to reality. Of course fairy tale material should not be given to the children in excess. We would further do well to let the children sense that this is just a tale and not something that really happened. A child who is prepared to believe will not be robbed of his belief, and the realists who always ask "is that true?" will be content with our frank answer that it is a fairy story, without thinking us untruthful. Susan Isaacs comes out openly on the side of the fairy tale and clearly contradicts the view held by Montessori and others. She writes: "Nor is the value of fairy tales in general in the least affected by the question of the truth about real events. No one who knows little children would wish to deprive them of the joys of the fairy-tales, as imaginative experience and literature, any more than one would wish to deprive the grown-up of imaginative art in painting and poetry and drama and the novel, because of the growth of scientific knowledge! We do not need to believe that the stories and plays are real historical truth in order to enjoy them. . . . And the little child goes on loving his fairy-stories, and having as much imaginative need of them when he understands true facts about real things. Indeed he can let his imagination roam all the more freely because his real life is rooted in truth and honesty. He is not for ever wondering whether what his parents say is true, and does not feel so perplexed about where the real ends and 'pretending' begins. . . . To share imaginative literature with the child, and to tell him untruth about real events, are two quite different things, which it is very important to distinguish."*

The most important objection to fairy-stories seems to me to be that they cause fear. It is certain that they may cause fear and affects, even lasting ones, in children with those tendencies. On the grounds of psychoanalytical experience it is assumed, however, that such fear will arise only where it is already present in the child's unconscious and where, in a way, it is just waiting for the opportunity to be directed on to a conscious object. In his account of an illness "From the History of an Infantile Neurosis"† Freud has given an example of this. There a fear leading to neurotic illness was apparently based on a dream connected with a frightening picture-book illustration of a wolf. During the analysis the fear of the wolf was shown to be only the cover for a real frightening experience.

Here is a case from my own experience. RENATE (aged 5) saw the fairy-tale play Little Red Riding Hood at the theatre. The very life-like wolf, who was much more frightening than the one in the tale, caused the child great fear, so that she wept and wanted to leave the theatre. From that day onwards RENATE was afraid of going into a dark room and did not dare to go into the dark corridor in her home. From hints given by the child it became gradually clear to me, that some time before she had been frightened by observations during the night in her parents' bedroom, which she had been reminded of by the wolf's attack. Fear had now found

* Susan Isaacs, op. cit., p. 121-122.
† Collected Papers (Hogarth Press, 1925) Vol. 3 p. 473.

a symbol and could be mentioned freely without her feeling ashamed; it could be talked about without RENATE knowing the cause of her fear.

As we have in general found from experience that conscious fear of a certain object has fewer damaging consequences than one that has been repressed in the unconscious, it remains an open question whether the release of a latent (29) fear is not an advantage. All the same I would not tell children fairy stories of which it can be expected beforehand they will alarm the child. Above all those popular with the children should be considered as first choice. A fairy-tale the child does not like should be avoided, for it must be assumed that the story is rejected because it touches too closely on unconscious conflicts. Children shy away from the awakening of painful thoughts, and they cannot bear it if they have to identify themselves with a fairy-tale character they dislike. The reason for this in each case is not clear, but the child's behaviour will tell us when to be considerate. Thus it was very noticeable when URSULA (aged 4), who loved fairy-tales otherwise, showed strong resistance and begun to cry when the other children wanted to hear "about the old woman who lived in a shoe". As soon as all settled down for the telling of a story, URSULA always begged fearfully "but not about the old woman who lived in a shoe"!

The example of URSULA proves how much more careful one has to be in the nursery school about telling stories than at home. Here the reaction of an individual child is more easily spotted than can be possible in a larger community. But there does not seem to me any reason to ban the fairy-tale, a source of great joy, from the nursery school, unless by exact psychoanalytical research results are reached which make this desirable. What I have tried to give here is more or less my own point of view. I cannot and do not want to lay down an absolute rule, but only hints to guide the reader towards an attitude of his own. Fairy-tales have remained popular with children for centuries, and all opposition of educationalists has not yet succeeded in abolishing them; this seems to me proof of how deeply children are attached to them.

It must not be overlooked that the teacher's own attitude to fairy tales will influence his point of view regarding them. Those who themselves loved fairy-tales in their childhood will hardly want children to be without them, although rationally there may be some objections. Emotional factors often give the lie to theories, and childhood memories cannot be wiped out with even the best intentions. Here I might also say a word in favour of Father Christmas—so often condemned by conscientious pedagogues. Just as fairy-tales are somehow picked up by children, although they may not have been told, so that one day they play a part in the child's life even without our encouragement—so it is with Father Christmas. Most children believe in him for a time and make him part of their fantasies. A child brought up by quite rational methods, in whose home Father Christmas did not exist, reported in the nursery school: "ANNE-MARIE's father met Father Christmas yesterday." These words were full of envious conviction. It is matter for thought that children—or at least so many of them—again and again show the desire to believe. When we hear the children's conversations among themselves just before Christmas, we ought to ask ourselves whether we should hold back from them something that they want so much and that seems in accordance with their nature.

Play and Occupations

Even if in relation to Father Christmas (and other symbolic figures) the child's general willingness to be fooled plays an important part, even if it can be assumed that Father Christmas is only a symbol to whom the child attaches his wishes, his hopes and also his fears— even so I would not want to remove him from the child's life. The Christmas daydreams should be allowed their right in any case. Do not let us clumsily destroy the child's dreams where they dare to appear, or impose our explanations where they were not asked for. Of course we should reply frankly and truthfully to the question whether there is such a thing as Father Christmas. For, where questions are asked doubt exists already and it is our task to end doubt.

Should we ourselves talk about Father Christmas, and pretend he exists when it means giving the children something to look forward to, excitement and hope? Should we give the children a pretence of Christmas and let Father Christmas come into the nursery school? I think we shall always do well to act according to what we feel. If we ourselves are still emotionally tied to an earlier experience of our own, we shall only with difficulty refrain from giving Christmas (and other holidays) a miraculous content for the children. If we have a more matter-of-fact outlook and are less close to the child's way of feeling, an attempt to present imaginary figures to the children would fail because of our own inability. It hardly needs saying that Father Christmas should never appear as an avenging power but only as a good and loving friend. In my own nursery school I allowed Father Christmas to be an imaginary figure but he never appeared in person—perhaps because I myself was once as a child terrified by such a disguise.

I will end our discussion of occupational methods in

the nursery school with a few hints on gymnastics and music; it has always been recognised that both are of importance in the child's education. The question is whether any new light can be shed from the psycho-analytical point of view on their function and usefulness. To penetrate this field and especially to find new values would need thorough researches, which have, as far as I know, either not been undertaken or not yet pub-lished. Experts in both subjects will have to place the results of psychoanalytical research at the disposal of this problem.

I shall confine myself to saying that it seems to me that modern gymnastics, which endeavour to increase body control by loosening-up exercises and tend to-wards a freer means of execution, have some points in common with psychoanalytical educational theory. Instead of influencing the child by strict discipline and force we attempt freely to initiate in the child an emo-tional equilibrium and to counteract faulty develop-ment and overpowerful tendencies to repression. Modern gymnastics have helped to emphasise the idea that every exercise and task must originate from the body itself. It seems most desirable for the method of gymnastics used to be in harmony with the principles guiding the conduct of the nursery school. Gymnastics must be a part of the whole of the nursery school—not something separate, but an expression of the psycholo-gical-pedagogic orientation. Thus bearing our principles in mind, in gymnastic exercises the exaggeration of am-bition and the creation of inferiority feelings must be avoided. On one hand an attempt should be made to create an emotional equilibrium for the children by exer-cises; on the other hand the individual child's unconscious attitude towards gymnastics should be taken into account and should be discovered if possible and used as a means of gaining more knowledge of the child's emotional life.

It is not for me to examine the use of music in the nursery school from the psychoanalytical point of view; nevertheless the serious effect which the premature use of faulty musical exercises may have on the child's emotional development must be mentioned. It is not disputed that artistic and intellectual talent varies according to individual constitutions, but on the basis of psychoanalytical knowledge it is claimed that many a child is counted among those without talent, when he does not deserve this label. This may be regarded as certain since the analysis of adults has shown how strongly inhibitions developed in earliest childhood tend to stifle the development of such talents. When such inhibitions have later been relieved by the discovery of their unconscious motives during analytical treatment, new fields of interest are opened up, especially the development of talents and artistic sensitivity. We must therefore conclude that if we can prevent the development of such inhibitions the number of the so-called "untalented" children will diminish. It hardly needs stressing that this would be of importance not only in relation to music but also to a person's general emotional development. Even though we have no absolute power in this direction, as we cannot be sure of excluding all inhibiting factors, we can still draw deductions from it for the development of music in the nursery school. *The practice of music is to be organised in such a way that no critical judgments are made on its performance.* It should be a joyful creativeness on the children's part and not a "showing off", as practised in most nursery school concerts. Achievement must not be the most important thing with such young children. The music

131

Psychology in the Nursery School

teacher, Heinrich Jacoby, once discussed the subject, "Must there be unmusical people?" from the psychoanalytical point of view.* One paragraph which seems of importance for the general treatment of the children's occupations in the nursery school is quoted here: "The conviction that one is thought without talent by all must further undermine the tottering structure of self-confidence. Finally the individual concerned will try more and more to avoid the demands of life which remind him of situations in which he has failed before. Therefore he will frequently produce, even though unconsciously, just those symptoms which caused him to be thought without talent in the beginning. If only because of the danger of such effects *all evaluation of talent should if possible, be avoided*".

* *Zeitschrift fur Psychoanalytische Pedagogik*, I. 35 and 110. (1926.)

CHAPTER VIII

THE NURSERY SCHOOL'S
RELATION TO PSYCHOANALYSIS

I have tried to view the nursery school from the standpoint of psychoanalytically orientated education and to show how it might thus be run. Now we must try to throw light on the direct relations between psychoanalysis and the nursery school. Perhaps it has already become evident from previous remarks that we are not only endeavouring to guide the nursery school child according to psychoanalytical theory but also to suggest that frequently psychoanalysis ought to work hand in hand with the nursery school.

Those who work in nursery schools know the difficulties created by the "problem child" in the successful conduct of the school. Too highly strung in the everyday sense of the word, "psychopathological" in the sense of general educational therapy, and "neurotic" in the psychoanalytical sense, these children not only make difficulties for the staff *they themselves have difficulties*. One of the greatest problems in nursery school education is how these children can be helped. In many cases they cannot do justice to themselves in a general nursery school; instead they need special guidance, sympathetic understanding of their peculiarities, fears and their frequent (only neurotic) mental inhibitions. This understanding is in their own interest as well as that of the other children whose harmonious community existence may be easily upset. These children with disturbed affects and instinctual lives do not belong in a crowd.

Special nursery schools conducted on psychological lines are essential to-day. Many faulty developments can be remedied by someone suitably qualified in charge or by a favourably organised, sympathetic environment without actual treatment; the child may be improved to such an extent that return to the ordinary nursery school is possible. It should, however, not be forgotten that in some cases single symptoms may disappear, but the actual psychic disturbance may continue, although the child's general behaviour has improved. We know now that in some cases of more serious neurotic illness* where difficulties are rooted in the unconscious, educational guidance alone or a mere change of environment are insufficient. It may lead to repressions that seem outwardly favourable, or to a settling down, or the child may be given a sense of security and results may be achieved by the establishment of a good transference relationship. Without wishing to minimise the value of these influences we must assume because of the experiences gained in adult analyses that we are dealing mainly with temporary successes here, not with the removal of the actual neurosis.

In suitable cases, to be determined by a psychiatrist, treatment would be the best thing. As far as the child's condition makes contact with other children desirable, the child should go into a special nursery school where this is possible, this in spite of the treatment, or rather because of it, as we shall show.

One of the tasks of the nursery school is to discover

---

* It is emphasised that psychic disturbances are not shown by "difficult" behaviour only, but that neurotic children are often particularly easily led. I am thinking of the "too good" inhibited child.

neurotic symptoms in good time by careful observation; thus the child's parents can be persuaded by our influence and explanations to give the child the best possible care and in certain circumstances should be informed that treatment is necessary.* In this connection it should once again be pointed out that we consider contact with parents an important duty of the person in charge of a nursery school. A teacher well trained in psychology and also experienced will not only use her knowledge for the children's benefit but will try to enlighten parents in private conversations, in interviews and perhaps by a lecture course. In cases of persistent bed-wetting, stealing, lying and similar symptoms mothers are often at a complete loss what to do and are grateful for help. In our consultations and attempts to enlighten we should not however forget that our proposals will only be accepted if good personal relations exist. Purely intellectual instructions usually cause resistance.

It has been mentioned that the mothers of children treated in child guidance clinics are given instructions in psychological matters at the same time. About this it is reported ". . . but even the worst of bad parents, whom we meet in child guidance clinics, respond to careful influence, and the average mother is prepared to adapt her treatment of the child to his needs as soon as she is made aware of them."† The realisation that treatment of the child is of little use unless the parents

* Although when mentioning treatment we are thinking of psychoanalysis or a dispersion of symptoms on psychoanalytical lines, it is realised that this is possible in only a very few cases. So the reader is advised to think of guidance bureaux, run on general psychological lines, in particular child guidance clinics, which if they cannot always do analysis can provide some other psychological treatment.

† Dr. R. MacCalman in his lecture, "Aggression in relation to Family Life", Int. Conference on Child Psychiatry, London, 1948.

are guided to a sympathetic point of view is spreading. It is not sufficient to teach child-psychology—however valuable this may be. Parents and especially mothers should be led on beyond this to understand their *own* problems or psychological complaints, as far as these seem capable of having a bad effect on their common life with their children. Nowadays there is a tendency in psychoanalytical circles to give the analysis of a neurotic mother precedence over that of the child who is causing the difficulties. Occasionally it will be the task of the nursery school teacher to point out the need of treatment to a mother, and to help her in finding a place where this can be done.

In order to anticipate misunderstandings let it be emphasised that *the children visiting a nursery school should never be analysed by the person in charge*, not even if she is psychoanalytically trained. To me at least it seems doubtful whether the life of the nursery school would not be much upset by the transference relationship, the giving of complete freedom essential to the analysis and the attitude of the analyst there, which must never resemble that of a teacher. It would of course be different and better for the children, if, as has been done in several places in the U.S.A., a psychiatrist specially employed for this task takes care of the difficult nursery school children. It seems probable to me that a nursery school teacher thoroughly trained in psychoanalysis may occasionally help mother or child by a frank and revealing talk and may be able to dissolve single symptoms; but superficial attempts at analysis by people who have no thorough knowledge of psychoanalysis must be avoided at all costs.

Perhaps it would not be out of place to point out here that according to my experience, although this is limited to a few cases only, difficulties will always occur in the nursery school while a child is receiving analytical treatment. For this very reason it is advisable to send any child who is in the middle of an analysis to a nursery school where at least the person in charge is versed in psychoanalysis. If the person in charge does not know anything about it, it may easily happen that intentionally or unintentionally she works against the analysis or does not know how to interpret the child's behaviour correctly and therefore reacts to it in an undesirable manner. The difficulties mentioned may for example occur if the child has transferred well (positively) to the person in charge until he is analysed and therefore, contrary to his behaviour in other places has been easily controlled and well adjusted to the nursery school in every respect. This was the case with ERNA, with whom I had the opportunity to observe the effects of analysis closely during the early months, especially as I was in constant contact with the analyst carrying out the treatment.

After about two weeks of analysis ERNA suddenly became very aggressive towards the other children, which she had never been before. Sometimes she hit other children without any visible cause and sometimes when she had been annoyed by something she became altogether very irritable. During my period of observation her aggressiveness diminished but never disappeared completely. Masturbation had also been practised before but increased noticeably. For a time the child masturbated constantly while at the nursery school. She pressed herself against the table, moving from side to side even while engaged in other occupations that interested her. After a few weeks masturbation became noticeable only occasionally.

Before her analysis ERNA did not play much but preferred to talk. On walks she walked only with me, talking without interruption. In a way she was playing the adult and thus keeping herself at a distance from other children. ERNA was very fond of talks with me alone in my room, telling me of her dreams and her daily problems. She was suffering from a kind of compulsive brooding, and sometimes worried for days about things she had heard. Soon after the analysis had begun she did not need me any longer to talk to about herself. Her excessive talking stopped altogether. She began to play by herself and with other children and became the close friend of a small girl whom she dominated. From the "little adult" a really naughty child developed gradually, though she had been so excessively obedient before that one could not help noticing it. Once for example she had dissolved into tears when I told all the children that they had been too noisy; now she made a point of breaking the rules of the nursery school. I had lost all influence over ERNA. Her strongly expressed transference relationship to me had ended completely and as this had been the basis of her behaviour in the nursery school, it was understandable that difficulties arose now.

It is not possible to describe the stages of the protacted analysis which brought about favourable changes in ERNA. Here it was clearly shown how the variations in a child's behaviour caused by analysis make their mark in a nursery school and how they demand attention.*

In another case I observed that the child LENI, completely changed her occupations in the nursery school in the course of her analysis. Before LENI had

* Further details of ERNA's analysis may be found in Melanie Klein's *Contributions to Psycho-analysis*, 1921–1945. Hogarth Press and Institute of Psycho Analysis.

been especially creative and had painted a great deal and well. Now, for a time at least, this interest had ended entirely. She refused to have any dealings with the nursery school occupations but played with dolls with the utmost concentration. Her urge to communicate had been expressed before in drawing, but it was now satisfied by the analysis and the content of her games seemed to be drawn from the subject of her analysis. With LENI I noticed the same as with ERNA: the transference on me ceased almost entirely and I thus lost my influence on the child. Conflicts arising in the community life of the nursery school I naturally dealt with quite otherwise than a teacher without analytical knowledge would have done.

One may already gather from these few examples how important it is for a child to be in a sympathetic environment while receiving analytical treatment, and a special nursery school run on such lines would do much good in this direction. Particularly where removal from an unsatisfactory domestic environment, as Anna Freud proposes,* is impossible, *temporary* absence from unsuitable family influence, that is a stay in a nursery school run with understanding of this problem, may be of advantage. Anna Freud imagines as desirable a school which "is guided by analytical principles and which is attuned to collaboration with the analyst". In agreement with my own experience Willie Hoffer points out that child analysis may at times have an anti-pedagogic effect, and impose a greater strain on the teacher than would the open untreated disturbance of the child which he tries to influence by purely disciplin-

* A. Freud. *Einführung in die Technik der Kinderanalyse.* Int. Psychoanal. Verlag. Wien, 1929, p. 59. ‡ p. 76. Eng. Edn.: *The Psycho-analytical Treatment of Children.* Imago Publishing Co., Ltd. London 1946. p. 36, ‡ p. 45.

ary measures.* While the child is in the charge of a nursery school teacher unacquainted with psycho-analytical principles, conflicts between child and teacher may easily occur.

Anna Freud speaks of joint work between teacher and analyst and thus wishes to avoid useless opposition of the two, or rather unnecessary duplication of effort; this requires further advice on our part. In such a case the teacher must be content to take second place, not because his work is of less importance, but because in this particular situation, i.e. during the analytical treatment, analysis and the analyst should stand above everything. "The analyst must succeed in putting himself in place of the child's ego-ideal for the duration of the analysis." The authority of the analyst must also therefore be recognised by the teacher and "the necessity for the child's complete domination by the analyst" must not be undermined by any personal rivalry. Otherwise the child, as I have had occasion to observe, is placed in a very awkward situation.

Of course, if fruitful collaboration is to be possible, teacher and analyst must exchange their information. Only then will it be possible for the nursery school to reduce to a minimum its mistakes in guiding the child and the analyst through the information supplied by a sympathetic teacher will get to know of some of the child's reactions and will be able to make good use of them.

* "Psychoanalytic Education", in *The Psychoanalytic Study of the Child.* Imago Publishing Co., Ltd. 1946. p. 298.

INDEX OF NAMES

INDEX OF SUBJECTS

141

Index

Behaviour, see Attitude, Good Child, Teacher
governed by emotional factors, 19
outward behaviour, 20, 28
family relationship as cause of, 23
when entering the nursery school, 25
easily guided in nursery school, 43

Case Histories, 21 (2), 22, 23, 40, 41, 46, 50 (3), 51 (2), 53, 58, 60, 61 (5), 64, 65 (2), 66 (3), 68 (2), 69, 72, 95, 103, 105 (3), 107, 108 (2), 109, 116, 119, 126, 127, 128, 137, 138
Castration complex, 46, 48
Child Guidance Clinics, 23, 135
Community, 38, 43, 77, 78, 80, 81
spirit, 35
organised interests, 42
equality in, 48
small groups, 85
community games, 103 ff.
Compensation, see Over-compensation

Daydreams, 25, 99. See Play
Depth-psychology, 39, 91, 113
Destruction
destructive wishes, 79
destructive activities, 121
Development, 25, 31, 98, 107, 131
urge to, 16, 102
delay of, 17
arrest of, 32
faulty, 49, 119
Difficulties
of children visiting Nursery School, 20
of teachers, 88, 90

Early experiences, 75
Education, see Psychoanalytical interference, 18, 41, 76, 78, 80, 89, 116
authoritarian manner, 40, 41, 81, 90

Education—cont.
educational theory of sex differentiation, 48
sex education, 54
educational measures, 76
freedom, 79–80
restrictions, 80
independence, 82, 83
aim of, 82
educational influence and unconscious, 109
educational toys, 114
Ego-ideal, 16, 81, 140

Fairy tales, 123 ff.
Father Christmas, 128 ff.
Family relations, see Jealousy, Oedipus Complex, Parents
attachment to parents, 31
liberation from close family ties, 33, 83
brothers and sisters, 34, 51
conflicts, 42, 78
brother-and-sister complex, 44
Fear and Anxiety, 26, 27, 105, 123, 124, 133
fear of going to school, 26
fear of loss of love, 86
fear of animals, 122
conscious and unconscious of, 127
Fixation, 62
Friendships, 41
erotically tinged, 63–76
influencing sexual life, 75
after-effects, 75
Frustration, 79

Games, see Play
"Good" child, 15, 38, 80
Guilt, feelings of, 16, 46, 81, 82, 89, 123
Gymnastics, 130 ff.

Habits, trying to break, 59

Identification, 43, 89, 124
Inferiority
feelings of, 16, 34, 46, 82, 123
teachers who feel inferior, 48
Inhibition, 18, 55, 131, 133

142

Index

Index